Migration and Skills

Migration and Skills

The Experience of Migrant Workers from Albania, Egypt, Moldova, and Tunisia

Jesús Alquézar Sabadie, Johanna Avato, Ummuhan Bardak,
Francesco Panzica, and Natalia Popova

ETF ★ Working together
Learning for life

THE WORLD BANK
Washington, DC

1818 H Street, NW
Washington, DC 20433
Telephone 202-473-1000
Internet www.worldbank.org
E-mail feedback@worldbank.org

1 2 3 4 :: 13 12 11 10

A publication of the World Bank in collaboration with the European Training Foundation (ETF).

ISBN: 978-0-8213-8079-6
eISBN: 978-0-8213-8119-9
DOI: 10.1596/978-0-8213-8079-6

Library of Congress Cataloging-in-Publication Data

Migration and skills : the experience of migrant workers from Albania, Egypt, Moldova and Tunisia / Jesús Alquézar Sabadie ... [et al.].
    p. cm. — (Directions in development)
  Includes bibliographical references and index.
  ISBN 978-0-8213-8079-6 (alk. paper) — ISBN 978-0-8213-8119-9
  1. Foreign workers—European Union countries. 2. Vocational qualifications. 3. Human capital—European Union countries. 4. European Union countries—Emigration and immigration—Government policy. I. Alquézar Sabadie, Jesús.
  HD8378.5.A2M538 2009
  331.5'44—dc22

2009032584

Contents

Figures

Tables

Foreword and Acknowledgments

The European Union (EU) is one of the world's most favored destinations for immigrants. Although security issues are foremost, EU policy is beginning to give increasing importance to the potential contribution that migration can make to development and the mutual benefits for both sending and receiving countries. In this context, the impact of migration on skills development and labor-market policies is a topic that both the European Training Foundation (ETF) and the World Bank are interested in exploring.

The policy reference point and context for the countries involved in this study (Albania, the Arab Republic of Egypt, the Republic of Moldova, and Tunisia) are the EU neighborhood and enlargement policies, which cover the eventual membership in the European Union of Albania and closer integration into the internal market for Egypt, Moldova, and Tunisia. The key question raised by the study is whether migration and skills are linked in a way that could contribute to the development of both the EU and the home country and, at the same time, benefit the migrant. Such a win-win-win situation would involve broad matches between skills supplied by migrants and the EU's need for skills, and between knowledge gained by migrants and the knowledge needs of their home countries.

To ensure that the supply of skills brought by migrants from their home countries meets skills shortages in the EU labor market, sending countries would need to have in place a quality assured certification system, and receiving countries would need to have in place mechanisms for the recognition of migrants' qualifications. To ensure that the know-how and experience brought back by returning migrants assists with their re-integration into their home labor market, meets business needs, and aids further development of the education and training system, the home countries would need to have mechanisms in place for the certification of skills and education, formal and informal, the migrants gained abroad.

This synthesis report is of particular interest because its analysis is original. It is based on ETF's survey database that compares two countries demonstrating traditional emigration patterns (Egypt and Tunisia) with two Eastern European transition countries (Albania and Moldova). In the latter, the migration phenomenon intertwines with overhauled economies—a period of decline followed by economic recovery—but jobless growth paradoxically coexists with observable labor or skill shortages in given sectors of the national labor markets. Separate country migration reports including the main findings of ETF surveys are already available and downloadable from the ETF website.

As the surveys were carried out by ETF in late 2006 and early 2007, well before the current economic crisis exploded, it is important to emphasize that the report does not provide information about how the global crisis is affecting migrants or its impact on the economies of sending countries.

This synthesis report was written by a team of ETF and World Bank staff. While ETF provided the background work and most policy discussions in the report, the World Bank presented the findings of their econometric analyses conducted with the survey data. The interinstitutional cooperation between the two organizations is a first of its kind and illustrates the importance of this topic for the economic and social development of both the sending and receiving countries around the Mediterranean. It should help to trigger more cooperation around this topic among other interested and involved partners.

We would like to express special thanks to Professor Richard Black, who worked on behalf of ETF in developing the survey methodology and provided input for this synthesis report together with ETF staff.

Madlen Serban
Director
European Training Foundation

Robert Holzmann
Director
Social Protection and Labor
World Bank

About the Authors

Jesús Alquézar Sabadie holds a degree in sociology and political science from the Universidad del País Vasco, as well as postgraduate diplomas in European politics (Université Libre de Bruxelles) and applied research techniques in social sciences (Centro de Investigaciones Sociológicas, Spain). Before joining the European Training Foundation (ETF) in 2007, he worked for the Centro de Investigaciones Sociológicas (Madrid), the Spanish Embassy's Economic and Commercial Office in Casablanca, Eurobarometer, and Eurydice, the information network on education in Europe. He currently provides statistical support at the ETF in the fields of labor markets, vocational education and training, gender, competitiveness, and migration.

Johanna Avato is an economist consulting for the World Bank's Human Development Network for Social Protection and Labor (HDNSP) in the field of international migration. She works primarily on migration and skills, and on the portability of social security rights for migrants. Before joining the World Bank, she was a visiting scholar at the Institute for the Study of International Migration at Georgetown University. She holds a PhD in economics from the University of Tübingen, Germany.

Ummuhan Bardak studied political science and international relations in Turkey and completed her master's degree at the London School of Economics. After working on employment policies at the Turkish Ministry of Labor for seven years, she currently works as a labor-market specialist at the ETF in Italy. She has worked on the ETF's Patterns of Migration and Human Resources Development project and the implementation of the Euro-Mediterranean Partnership's (MEDA) Education and Training for Employment (ETE) program. She is currently involved in a labor-market review of the Black Sea countries (Armenia, Azerbaijan, Belarus, Georgia, Moldova, and Ukraine), a study on "flexicurity" and lifelong learning, and a MEDA study on employability.

Francesco Panzica holds degrees in law, archaeology, contemporary history, and international studies from Turin University in Italy. He worked as a civil servant with the Municipality of Turin before joining the ETF in 1994. An experienced project manager, he has a personal interest in the role of vocational education and training for local economic development, social inclusion, and employment generation. He has extensive experience in project design, implementation, and monitoring, and with the implementation of EU assistance projects in different countries. He was a member of the Organisation for Economic Co-operation and Development (OECD) Education Review Team for Albania and has worked with the OECD on local economic and employment development in Albania and Kosovo, and on an informal economy analysis in Albania.

Natalia Popova has worked on labor-market issues, including providing support to the European Commission (EC) for project design and implementation in the field of labor-market and vocational-education reforms for the Western Balkans since July 2004. In 2006, she began working on the links between labor migration and education and training systems. Before joining the ETF, she worked for the International Labour Organization (ILO) in Geneva as a research economist. She has also worked on short-term assignments for the World Trade Organization (WTO) and the United Nations Economic Commission for Europe (UNECE). She holds a master's degree in international trade and commercial diplomacy from the Monterey Institute of International Policy Studies, California.

Overview

The subject of migration, and how best to manage it, has been moving up the policy agenda of the European Union for some time now. Faced with an aging population, possible skills shortages at all skills levels, and the need to compete for highly skilled migrants with countries such as Australia, Canada, and the United States, the EU is moving from seeing migration as a problem or a threat to viewing it as an opportunity.

As an EU agency promoting skills and human capital development in transition and developing countries, the ETF wished to explore the impact of migration on skills development, with a special emphasis on diasporas and returning migrants.[1] For the World Bank, the issue of migration forms an integral part of its approach to social protection, since it believes that labor-market policy must take into account the national as well the international dimensions of skilled labor mobility. Both institutions were keen to look at what changes need to be made to migration policy in order to achieve a triple-win situation, one that can benefit both sending and receiving countries as well as the migrants themselves.

This report aims to unravel the complex relationship between migration and skills development. It paints a precise picture of potential and returning migrants from four very different countries—Albania, the Arab Republic of Egypt, Moldova, and Tunisia—that is a conscious choice of two "traditional"

(Egypt, Tunisia) and two "new" (Albania, Moldova) sending countries, and describes the skills they possess and the impact that the experience of migration has on their skills development. By doing so, it aims to promote a better understanding of the phenomenon of migration and the human faces behind it—who they are and what they can offer, to the countries to which they migrate and to their countries of origin when they return.

The report is based upon extensive field surveys carried out at the end of 2006 and beginning of 2007. The target groups were 1,000 potential migrants—defined as young adults between 18 and 40 living in the country—and 1,000 returned migrants in each country. This second group was defined as adults ages 18 and over who had lived and worked abroad for at least 6 months and who had returned to their countries of origin within the last 10 years. People were interviewed in their homes using a standard questionnaire. In the case of returning migrants, people who had migrated both legally and illegally were included, although the questionnaire did not specifically address this issue.

The analysis covers a wide range of issues. The first section looks at segments of the population that intended to migrate and which kinds of people were most likely to do so. It analyzes how factors such as age, gender, marital status, and language skills affect this decision, and explores what part education has to play. Interestingly, with the exception of Egypt, the data show that it is not predominantly the highly skilled who intend to migrate. It found that respondents with very different levels of educational attainment showed a similar level of interest in migrating.

People's current status in the labor market, however, was found to have a big impact. In all four countries, unemployed people, students, and casual laborers were those most likely to be thinking of migrating, and people working in low-skilled jobs were more likely to intend to migrate than those with higher-level skills. Nevertheless, the numbers of professionals and managers who intended to migrate was still significant; above 30 percent in all four countries and 41 percent (professionals) and 54 percent (managers) in Tunisia. This finding would seem to suggest that simply having a job, or even having a supposedly good job, does not prevent people from migrating, but that decent jobs, with good salaries and conditions, are the key to reducing the desire to migrate.

When it comes to choosing a migration destination, existing patterns of migration were very influential. Thus, Albanians and Tunisians were most likely to consider migrating to the EU, almost 60 percent of Egyptians were thinking of the Persian Gulf and a third of Moldovans were considering moving to Russia. The level of education also influenced the choice of destination; generally the more educated the potential migrants, the less likely they were to be planning to migrate to the EU. Many preferred the United States or Canada or, in the case of Egyptians, the Gulf. This finding was backed up by the link between current job status and the choice of destination; professionals and managers were those most likely to be considering a country outside the EU. The data also confirm the importance of social networks and established diasporas in people's choice of a migration destination.

In terms of preparation for migration, more than a third of potential migrants expressed an interest in training before they left, with language training the most popular option. However, in practice, this training is either not available or people do not take it up; only 5 percent of returned migrants had undertaken any form of predeparture training.

Unsurprisingly, there was a strong correlation between people's level of skills and the kind of job they hoped to find abroad, although there were differences between nationalities. Potential migrants from Moldova were the most likely to be expecting to do unskilled work, regardless of their skills, while Tunisians had the highest aspirations; many with low skills were expecting to find at least a skilled job abroad.

It is harder to draw accurate conclusions on the link between job aspirations and current employment status, since many of the potential migrants were not actively employed at the time of the interview. However, the data suggest people did expect to change jobs as a result of migration, and the sectors they expected to work in varied according to their nationality. Focusing solely on those planning to move to the EU, many Albanians expected to work in domestic service, hospitality, and construction; Egyptians expected to work in hospitality and construction; Moldovans expected to work in domestic service and construction; Tunisians expected to work in hospitality and manufacturing. Few migrants working in agriculture or petty trade aimed to work in these same sectors while abroad.

This last finding comes as no surprise, but the expectations of professionals and managers were more remarkable. About a third of these expected to work at a lower level as migrants. This could indicate that, in spite of their theoretically good jobs at home, they believe working conditions were considerably better abroad even if this meant accepting a lower-skilled job.

Data from returned migrants give an indication about the extent to which migrants fulfilled their expectations. An initial finding is that the jobs held by migrants abroad were more likely to be in agriculture or construction than expected. However, the short-term nature of employment in these sectors means this finding may be a result of selection bias. How far the reality of employment lived up to expectations also varied according to nationality; for instance, many Egyptians expected to work in public administration and, for most, this did turn out to be the case. There was little job mobility while abroad. Only 28 percent of migrants changed jobs, and 90 percent of those who started in unskilled or skilled occupations remained there.

The report also examines the extent to which migrants were able to use their skills and training while abroad, and thus whether their experiences are an example of brain gain or brain waste. It found that educated Egyptians fared best; many occupied posts as professionals and managers while abroad. Albanian and particularly Moldovan migrants fared the worst; more than 60 percent worked abroad as unskilled workers regardless of their qualifications. Tunisians occupied an intermediate position; more than 81 percent worked abroad as skilled or unskilled workers, including 37.5 percent who were classified as highly educated. Educated women did worse than educated men, especially if they migrated to work in the EU. For instance, 80 percent of Moldovan women with university degrees found only unskilled jobs, compared to 60 percent of Moldovan men with degrees. More than 55 percent of migrants to the EU found only unskilled work, and only 7.2 percent worked as managers or professionals. Thus the survey detected a significant waste of migrants' skills, especially for Albanians and Moldovans and, to a lesser extent, for Tunisians.

Migrants have an impact on the development of their countries of origin in two main ways: by sending money home and by rejoining the labor market on their return. Remittances from migrants play an important role in the economies of the four countries surveyed. In 2008, they represented 36 percent of GDP for Moldova and 15 percent for Albania, 4.3 percent for Egypt, and 5 percent for Tunisia, according to the World Bank. However most of the money migrants send home is used for immediate consumption; only a small proportion is channeled into income-generating activities. About three-quarters of returning migrants had sent remittances home while working abroad, according to the ETF survey. However, most of this money was used for living expenses—between 84 percent in Albania and just over 95 percent in Moldova.

Returning migrants also contribute to local development by rejoining the workforce or becoming entrepreneurs, but the study shows that this works better if certain conditions are met. Migrants need to have spent enough time abroad to accumulate sufficient human and financial capital but to still be of an age where they are willing to undertake new projects on their return. The return is likely to be more beneficial for the home country when individuals choose to return rather than are forced to do so. Finally, home countries can benefit more from the return of skilled migrants than unskilled ones as long as local conditions allow them to make good use of their skills on their return.

However, the survey showed that these conditions were not always met. For instance, most reasons given for return were either negative—one in five Tunisians reported they had been "sent away by the authorities"— or neutral, such as family reasons. Only a minority said they returned for positive reasons, such as starting a business.

Skills acquired abroad did have a positive impact on migrants' employability on their return; nearly 90 percent of those employed as professionals abroad worked after returning home, compared to less than 60 percent of people who worked in unskilled occupations. Only a low proportion of returnees worked in the same jobs on their return that they had held while abroad—just 35.5 percent. Many had moved into the sectors of commerce and petty trade—the preferred sectors for returning migrants who set up their own businesses. The survey shows that these entrepreneurial activities were more closely linked to the migrants' general experience while abroad than specific skills acquired on the job. Many migrants said their most useful experience while abroad was being exposed to new ways of doing things, rather than formal training or skills acquired at work.

All four countries surveyed have reasonably comprehensive policies on migration, although in Egypt and Tunisia, with their far longer tradition of emigration, these tend to be more developed. All strive to maintain and strengthen links with their diasporas as a way of fostering local development by attracting human and financial capital acquired abroad. All four have various emigration agreements with some of their receiving countries—once again, Egypt and Tunisia to a greater extent than Albania and Moldova—but the report finds these are largely ineffective. Only 10 percent of returning migrants knew of the existence of government schemes to support migration, and only 5.4 percent had made use of them.

The authors find there is a lack of effective ways to channel temporary skilled migration to the EU in all countries surveyed. Organized schemes that could match skills levels to demand are particularly lacking. In their absence, existing migration tends to follow market incentives, and migrants largely use informal channels. The authors call for migrants to be better prepared for migration through measures such as dedicated centers that provide advice on how to get their qualifications recognized in receiving countries or referral centers to put would-be migrants in touch with suitable expatriates. In the longer term, migrants would benefit from general moves to improve the quality of basic education and training, and develop adult education.

As mentioned earlier, the survey found that migrants' skills often were not put to good use while they were working abroad. This was especially true in the case of migrants working in the EU and affected Albanians and Moldovans to a greater extent than Egyptians and Tunisians. Although the jury is still out on why this should be so, the authors suggest several reasons for what it calls the brain waste. These include the nature of demand for labor in receiving countries, the lack or inefficient implementation of bilateral agreements to manage the flow of migrants, problems related to the quality of education in sending countries, and whether the qualifications they produce are recognized by receiving countries. The report also finds that the EU is a less attractive destination for highly skilled migrants than Canada or the United States. This could have serious consequences for the EU's long-term competitiveness.

The results of the survey show that, when it comes to returning migrants, most use informal channels to organize their return. Only a small proportion of the returning migrants interviewed had heard of the existence of government programs offering incentives to return, and even fewer—just 1 percent overall—had benefited from such schemes. The exception to the rule was Tunisia, where the government has made special efforts to maintain links with its diaspora and encourage people to return.

The findings of the report show that skilled migrants tend to fare better than unskilled migrants on their return and can deliver more benefits to the local economy. This would seem to support the case for promoting temporary skilled migration to the EU; however, the reality is far from this. On the one hand, there is an emphasis on encouraging less-skilled workers to return home, coupled with a tacit acceptance that skilled workers are likely to remain. On the other side, the evidence shows that home countries need to do much more to encourage their migrants to return and to facilitate a more productive use of their remittances, savings, and skills.

Both the EU and sending countries must do more to facilitate the recognition of migrants' qualifications. This is especially true for people coming to the EU to work, because it is one of the ways to prevent them from being employed in jobs below their capacity. It is also true for returning migrants, who currently find the skills and knowledge they have acquired while abroad have no formal currency in their countries of origin. Measures suggested include pilot actions to enable bilateral recognition of qualifications in priority sectors such as construction, agriculture, or nursing. However, care must be taken that these actions do not remain isolated examples, but instead act as forerunners for a more systemic approach to recognizing qualifications.

Note

1. The ETF helps transition and developing countries harness the potential of their human capital through the reform of education, training and labor-market systems in the context of the EU's external relations policy. These countries fall into three groups: pre-Accession region (Albania, Croatia, the former Yugoslav Republic of Macedonia, Turkey, Serbia, Bosnia and Herzegovina, Kosovo [as defined by the United Nations Security Council Resolution 1244 of 10 June 1999, hereinafter Kosovo], and Montenegro); countries of the EU Neighborhood region (Algeria, Armenia, Azerbaijan, Belarus, the Arab Republic of Egypt, Georgia, Israel, Jordan, Lebanon, Libya, the Republic of Moldova, Morocco, Occupied Palestinian Territories, the Russian Federation, the Syrian Arab Republic, Tunisia, and Ukraine); and the countries covered by the Development Cooperation Instrument (in particular Kazakhstan, the Kyrgyz Republic, Tajikistan, Turkmenistan, and Uzbekistan).

CHAPTER 1

Introduction

Background and Motivation

Migration, and particularly inward migration, is at the top of the agenda for most European countries. When migration arises in political debates, the most visible issue is security (including border controls, the fight against illegal flows, and expulsions). Despite the negative image of migration that is often portrayed, migrants have been contributing to the economies of many European countries. Europe still needs, and will continue to need, migrants in the future, as a result of the demographic challenge and the increasing global competition for human capital (Holzmann and Münz 2004). With an aging population and fertility rates under two,[1] current population levels will only be maintained or increased with the aid of inward migration (Koettl 2005). For instance, in Spain the population increased by 13.1 percent between 2000 and 2008 as a consequence of inward migration from other countries.[2] Such demographic expansion has been accompanied by economic growth, to which migrants have contributed. With the current demographic challenge, local labor markets alone would be unable to sustain economic expansion without inward migration. This applies to other EU countries besides Spain, in particular those in southern Europe and others such as Ireland and Finland (OECD 2004).

The EU area is one of the main labor-receiving regions in the world, with North America and Australia. With increasing migration pressures from around the world, and the demographic changes taking place in Europe, migration has become a political issue at the European level as well. The Amsterdam Treaty opened the door for a common EU immigration and asylum policy and, in effect, from 1999 gave the European Commission powers to create a common policy in the management of migratory flows. Another recent factor is the interaction between migration and the employment and social policies in the EU, in particular the role of migration in relation to the Lisbon objectives in the context of increasing skill and labor shortages. The conclusions of the Tampere, Seville, and Hague European Councils established the basis for an emerging immigration and asylum policy structured around four axes:

- the integration of migration policy into the EU's relationships with developing countries and the building of partnerships with countries of origin;
- the efficient management of migration flows through a comprehensive approach that includes both combating illegal migration and finding channels for legal migration;
- better integration of third-country nationals who have been legally residing and working in the EU;
- a common European asylum policy.

Although a cursory review of programs and activities suggests that there is an overwhelming concern for security, there is a growing emphasis on migration management in positive terms, on its contribution to local development, and on the identification of mutual benefits of collaborating with transition and developing countries.[3] EU policy on cooperation with transition and developing countries aims to improve their capacity for migration management and refugee protection, to prevent and combat illegal migration, to provide information on legal channels for migration, to build border-control capacity, to enhance document security, and to address the problem of return. In fact, the issue of migration has been gradually incorporated into all association and cooperation agreements since 1999, and the European Union has already allocated funds to assist transition and developing countries in their efforts to better manage migratory flows.[4]

The 2006 EC Communication on the creation of a new thematic program on migration for the period 2007–2013 once again confirmed the strategic importance of migration for the external relations of the EU.[5] The migration and development nexus has been increasingly referred to in EC documents as a potential area of cooperation with transition and developing countries, as seen in the EC Communication of 2002,[6] followed by a specific EC Communication on migration and development in 2005.[7] The latter mentions facilitating the transfer of workers' remittances to home countries by reducing costs and promoting their use for development, supporting the voluntary return and professional and socioeconomic reintegration of migrants at home, encouraging the contribution of diasporas to the socioeconomic development of home countries, mitigating brain drain and promoting brain circulation (including through appropriate forms of temporary migration), and building capacities for better management of migration.

The EU also actively participates in the United Nations' High-Level Dialogue on Migration and Development.[8] In all these developments there has been a shift from "more development for less migration" to "better managing migration for more development," and a greater emphasis on the developmental impact of migration for home countries, particularly through returning migrants, diasporas, remittances, and temporary migration as a remedy for brain drain. The EU has already demonstrated the need to take a proactive approach toward legal migration for employment purposes in its Communication on immigration, integration, and employment, and in the Green Paper on the management of economic migration. The results of a public debate on the Green Paper led to the adoption of the EC Communication on a policy plan on legal migration, which contains a roadmap for a whole range of legislative and nonlegislative measures.[9]

Recent EC Communications[10] clarify further key aspects of the comprehensive European migration policy that is emerging at the EU level, which is intended to tackle illegal migration, support legal migration, and build cooperation with transition or developing countries. The EC Communication on circular migration and mobility partnerships between the EU and neighboring countries[11] opens the way for new forms of temporary legal migration schemes to facilitate labor mobility. This also applies to some new directive proposals,[12] in particular, one concerning the "blue card" immigration system for highly skilled migrants, which is loosely based on the United States green-card scheme and which offers a two-year renewable work permit available throughout the EU.[13] Although it includes a number of restrictions (potential migrants would have to have a recognized qualification and three years' professional work experience, as well as a job offer that could not be filled by an EU citizen) and is likely to be subject to opt-outs from some countries (the United Kingdom and Ireland are likely to pursue their own points-based system and green-card schemes respectively), this proposal indicates significant policy development within Europe on the facilitation of legal temporary migration to the EU. The idea appears to be to move toward a more selective, and also possibly temporary, migration system involving cooperation between the EU and neighboring countries.[14]

Another EC Staff Working Document of 2008 on the common immigration policy for Europe[15] attempts to summarize a comprehensive analysis of the situation (definition of the problem and the main political orientations and objectives) at the EU level. In the meantime, the European Commission has made efforts to harmonize interventions for the integration of transition and developing country nationals into the European Union. On the education of migrants' children, Directive 77/486/CEE represented an early attempt to take action. The commission has recently presented a new Green Paper on the integration of children of migrant families in the EU education systems,[16] with the aim of providing an analysis of, and feeding the debate on, the challenges to education systems posed by increased inward migration. This can be considered a follow-up to "A Common Agenda for Integration: a framework for the integration of third-country nationals into the European Union,"[17] which was put forward by the Commission in 2005 and which proposed measures to put into practice the Common Basic Principles on Integration (CBPs).[18] On June 18, 2008, the European Parliament approved a directive on the return of illegal immigrants aimed at harmonizing rules and procedures in this field, giving a large degree of flexibility to member states.[19]

In conclusion, a policy change toward circular migration (temporary and selective inward migration, according to the needs of the European labor market) can be observed at the EU level. The first mobility partnership launched between the EU and Moldova is a recent case in point.[20] In this context, it becomes important to have information on the skills profile of potential and returning migrants, and the content and quality of the education and training systems in sending countries. New knowledge must be produced on the skills available and/or gained from migration in those countries at different levels, together with an impact assessment on local labor-market needs. The EU's multidimensional approach mentioned above requires different types of information and action in the field of migration. The developmental impact of migration in general, and the skills development[21] impact of migration in particular, become an issue for research and action. As an EU agency promoting skills and human capital development policies in transition and developing countries, the ETF is interested in a further exploration of the impact of migration on skills development (with a special focus on returning migrants and diasporas). The World Bank considers migration in the context of its social protection approach, where labor-market policies must take into account the national as well international dimension of skilled labor mobility. In light of increasing relevance of skilled labor migration, further analytical work is necessary in this field. This has been also increasingly linked to the employment and development policies to which a pool of donors has manifested its commitment.

In view of these developments, the ETF launched a pilot study in 2006 on the links between migration and the education and training systems in four ETF partner countries: Albania, Egypt, Moldova, and Tunisia. The four countries included in this study have diverse migration histories, as well as significant differences in their current patterns of migration. Two—Egypt and Tunisia—have long histories of migration, and in the case of Egypt, to the Gulf states, especially Saudi Arabia. In contrast to these traditional emigration countries, the two eastern European countries of Albania and Moldova have relatively recent experience of large-scale outward migration. Particularly in Albania, outward migration was virtually nonexistent between the end of the World War II and the fall of the Communist regime in 1990. However, since the collapse of Communism, and especially since the economic and political crises in the late 1990s, both countries have witnessed unprecedented outward migration flows. Thus, over the last 15 years or so, as many as 1 million people (25 percent of the country's population) have left Albania, mostly for neighboring Greece and Italy, but also for elsewhere in the EU and beyond.[22] Meanwhile, at least 600,000 people left Moldova during the same period (about one in six Moldovans) and are now living abroad in the EU and Russia (Pantiru, Black, and Sabates-Wheeler 2007). As will be shown later in this report, these different stories have strong implications on current migration patterns.

When analyzing migration figures, some caution is necessary. First, it is important to note that accurate figures for migration flows are largely absent for all four countries, with data for illegal migrants and returnees particularly difficult to collect. This in turn gives rise to widely varying estimates of total migration stocks for the four countries—from 280,000 to 600,000 in Moldova (CBS-AXA 2005), and from 2.5 million (Collyer 2004) to 5 million in Egypt (Saleh 2006). It should also be noted that in Tunisia, official estimates generally focus on the number of Tunisians who are registered at Tunisian consulates abroad, a figure that substantially overestimates Tunisian migration, as it includes second, third, and even fourth generations who were born overseas and hold other nationalities, but still wish to retain their ties to Tunisia. A global analysis of census figures for 2001 suggests a rather smaller number of Tunisians abroad—380,000[23] rather than 900,000—although this does not include Tunisians in the Gulf, where census figures on foreign-born populations are unavailable.

Nonetheless, it is clear that international migration has become a significant feature for all the countries in this study, and that a major part of this migration in all four cases is now directed toward the EU. All four countries have experienced both "temporary" and more "permanent" flows, with individuals moving both legally and illegally. In Moldova in particular, migration still appears to be a growing phenomenon. In contrast, migration in Albania appears to have peaked, while in Egypt and Tunisia migration opportunities have declined in recent years, and return migration also has been occurring (McCormick and Wahba 2003; Mesnard 2004).

Objectives of the Study

If estimating existing levels of migration to the EU is problematic, making predictions on future migration levels is clearly even more difficult. There are two standard approaches to this question. The first is to seek to model future flows based on past patterns, taking into account changes in factors such as GDP and unemployment rates in source and destination countries. Thus, studies of potential movement from Central and Eastern European countries to the EU15 following accession have typically suggested that about 3–4 percent of their population will move to the EU15 within a decade, representing some 3 to 4 million people, or about 1 percent of the total EU15 population (Alvarez-Plata, Brücker, and Siliverstovs 2003; Zaiceva 2006). However, such studies have to date been largely focused on EU accession states, rather than countries in the broader "European neighborhood."[24]

An alternative approach is to conduct surveys in potential migrant-sending countries, asking individuals directly if they intend to migrate, and if so when, how, and to where. A number of such studies have been conducted since the mid- to late-1990s across Central and Eastern Europe, with some showing quite alarming numbers of people considering migration to the EU and elsewhere. One of the most comprehensive, conducted by the International Organization for Migration (IOM), surveyed 1,000 individuals in 11 Central and Eastern European countries in 1998, and showed percentages ranging from 7 (in Bulgaria) to 26 (in the former Yugoslavia) who expressed an interest in migrating permanently, figures that rose to between 18 percent (in Poland) and 57 percent (in Croatia) when individuals were asked whether they would like to live and work abroad for a few years only (Wallace 1998). A more recent study in Bulgaria reported that 15 percent of the population planned to leave the country to work abroad for more than a year, with the proportion being twice as high for men as for women (Rangelova and Vladimirova 2004). A similar study in Latvia reported that 10 percent of the population had a high probability of going abroad to work within the next two years, with the intention to leave being higher among ethnic Russians than ethnic Latvians (Ivlevs 2007). Meanwhile, successive studies in Albania indicated that 38 percent of the population were "definitely planning to migrate" in 1992, with 29 percent planning to do so in 1998 (Kule et al. 2000).

However, such studies should be treated with caution, since the responses from individuals are highly sensitive to the questions asked, which are often different, and to the context within which they are asked, which is usually hypothetical. Indeed, an early study of potential migration from four Central and Eastern European countries by Heinz Fassmann and colleagues in 1996 (Fassman and Hintermann 1997) distinguished between "general migration potential," where 30 percent of respondents expressed a desire to emigrate, and "real migration potential," where the proportion fell to just 1–2 percent, these being individuals who had already applied for a work permit, looked for somewhere to live, or begun looking for a job.

The ETF decided to follow this second approach in its pilot project on migration and skills in Albania, Egypt, Moldova, and Tunisia. Albania and Moldova were chosen as recent cases of emigration, while Egypt and Tunisia were selected as countries with a long tradition of emigration that will continue in the future. In 2006, the ETF launched a pilot study on the links among migration, the education and training system, and the labor market. Because knowledge relating to the overall consequences of migration in relation to education and skills and the labor market is limited, the ETF research approach targeted both potential and returning migrants, and included a review of existing literature, fact-finding missions, field surveys carried out with about 2,000 people in each country, and an analysis of the survey data.[25]

The main objective of the ETF study was to explore the link between migration and human capital development. This topic has not always been taken into account in migration literature, particularly in surveys, although interest is currently growing.[26] The education and skills of migrants are nevertheless crucial issues for the development of migration policies in the EU and for achieving an optimal "win-win-win" situation for all the parties involved in the migration process (home countries, host countries, and migrants themselves).

Hence, the following topics and issues are explored in this document:

- The characteristics of migration flows are described, and migration profiles for the countries surveyed established. An analysis is made of the educational level of migrants and its influence on the decision to migrate, the destination country, job expectations, and experiences abroad, among other factors.

- Migration can lead to "brain drain" or, even worse, to "brain waste." The ETF survey helps to identify the extent to which migration implies a skills match or mismatch, and the factors that influence such use (or misuse) of human capital. The role of qualification recognition and the use of transparency tools for the skills of migrants acquired at home or abroad are analyzed.

- Migration can have a positive effect on home-country development. The most commonly cited benefit is that of remittances sent by migrant workers while they are abroad. This document discusses the pros and cons of remittances, the factors that influence sending behavior of remittances, and in particular the way in which the money is used in the home country. A second major way in which international migration is thought to benefit home countries is through the return of migrants, provided this leads to the transfer of financial, human, or social capital. The use of savings and of skills acquired or developed abroad is analyzed, with a strong emphasis on the entrepreneurial activities of returning migrants.

The information provided in this joint ETF-World Bank report is based largely on the results of ETF field surveys in the four countries concerned, but the existing and possible future migration policies of the countries also are brought into the discussion. These include

- instruments to support organized migration to the benefit of the source country, the host country, and migrants themselves, including circular migration;

- policy options for mitigating the negative effect of brain drain and brain waste;
- the potential contribution of national and international organizations on local development of the home countries;
- possible partnerships between the EU and the home countries.

Methodology

The preliminary ETF study included a review of the existing literature, fact-finding missions, and field surveys in four ETF partner countries: Albania, Egypt, Moldova, and Tunisia,[27] during November and December 2006. Some of these countries are new sources of migration to the EU, and some are traditional sources. The survey methodology was almost the same in all the countries covered by the study. Common questionnaires and sampling were developed by the ETF and an international expert, Professor Richard Black, director of the Sussex Centre for Migration Research in the United Kingdom. In each country a local company was contracted to carry out the field survey and the first level of data analysis.

Two target groups were included in the field survey: potential migrants and returning migrants. It was anticipated that 1,000 potential migrants and 1,000 returning migrants would be interviewed in each country. The fieldwork consisted of face-to-face interviews carried out at respondents' households, using a written questionnaire. Only one person from each household was selected for the interview.[28] Two separate questionnaires (see annex 3) and sampling techniques were developed and implemented for potential and returning migrants, respectively.

A potential migrant was defined as anyone age 18–40 years who lived in the country at the moment of the interview. The survey on potential migration was intended to be broadly representative of the young adult population (18–40 years) in each country, in order to have a control sample of those in the same age group who were not actively seeking to migrate.

A returning migrant was someone who

- left the survey country at age 18 or older
- lived and worked abroad continuously for at least six months
- returned at least three months before the interview and within the previous 10 years
- was present during the fieldwork and available for interview

Those who had returned within the past three months or more than 10 years ago were not included in the survey.

A two-stage cluster sample was selected. First-stage clusters were a minimum of four to six regions chosen to represent the geographical diversity of the country, and second-stage clusters were villages, towns, or municipalities chosen to represent the geographical diversity of the selected regions. The procedure for selecting individual interviewees varied for potential migrants and returning migrants. Potential migrants' households were selected by interviewers following random routes, while returning migrants were identified and selected by local companies using the "snowball" sampling technique.[29]

Details on sampling design, problems encountered during the fieldwork, and a complete assessment of data representativeness are provided in annex 1. The following biases and representativeness problems must be taken into account before analyzing the results of the survey.

- **Gender bias.** In Egypt, Tunisia, and, to a lesser extent, Albania, fewer women than men were interviewed. This scenario was expected for the returning migrants' survey, but not particularly for potential migrants. This is mainly due to cultural reasons and to the nature of the migration phenomenon in these national contexts.
- **Education bias.** Compared with census statistics in each country, educated people tended to be overrepresented and individuals with low levels of education were underrepresented. This is the result of fieldwork problems. Despite the fact that the selection of an interviewee within a household was intended to be a random choice, it is likely that the highest-educated individuals preferred to answer.
- **Age bias.** Not surprisingly, young people (who are generally more educated) were also overrepresented.
- **Returning migrants.** The "snowball' sampling technique is not a probabilistic one.

It is also important to underscore that both legal and illegal returning migrants were interviewed. They were not directly asked whether they migrated legally or illegally, but the questionnaire provides some indications about this (through the questions about the reasons to return to the home country, which include answers such as "laid off by authorities" or the variable of whether someone paid social security benefits in the host country). In any case, it is important to keep in mind that the fact of migrating legally or illegally has strong implications on the topics analyzed in the joint ETF-WB report.

Another important point that must be taken into account concerns the timing of the study. Survey fieldwork was carried out during November and December 2006, well before the current worldwide economic crisis. The implication of the crisis on migrants, who are generally the most fragile part of host country societies, and on the development of the sending countries, are not covered by evidence provided through the surveys.

The data were analyzed in two complementary ways: Through (1) simple correlation tables and (2) econometric models. The tables describe the data in detail, and the econometric analysis allows the relevant correlations of the variables of interest to be examined while other variables are held constant at their mean.

Notes

1. According to Eurostat 2006 data (http://epp.eurostat.ec.europa.eu), the fertility rate is defined as the average number of children a woman will have in her lifetime. Only France had a fertility rate of 2, while Ireland, the United Kingdom, and the Nordic countries had rates between 1.83 and 1.9. Countries such as Spain, Italy, Germany, and Poland, among others, had rates below 1.4.

2. Eurostat (http://epp.eurostat.ec.europa.eu).

3. A "balanced approach," as described in Cassarino 2006.

4. The budget heading B7-667 for the period 2001–2003 (a total budget of €42.5 million), and AENEAS program for 2004–2006 (a total budget of €250 million), based on the EC Regulation No.491/2004 of 10.3.2004 establishing a program for financial and technical assistance to developing countries in the areas of migration and asylum.

5. EC Communication on the creation of a new thematic program and budget for cooperation with third countries in the areas of migration and asylum within the Financial Perspectives 2007–13, 25.01.2006, COM26.

6. EC Communication on integrating migration issues in the EU's relations with third countries, COM(2002) 703 final, 03.12.2002.

7. EC Communication on migration and development: some concrete orientations, COM(2005) 390 final, 01.09.2005.

8. See EC Communication on the EU position for the United Nations' High-Level Dialogue on Migration and Development, COM(2006) 409 final, 14.07.2006. The last conference was held September 14–15, 2006, in New York.

9. See EC Communication on immigration, integration and employment, COM(2003) 336 final, 03.06.2003; EC Green Paper on an EU approach to managing economic migration COM(2004) 811 final, 11.01.2005; and

EC Communication on a policy plan on legal migration SEC(2005)1680, COM(2005) 669 final, 21.12.2005.

10. EC Communication on global approach to migration one year on: towards a comprehensive European migration policy, COM(2006) 735 final, 30.11.2006; EC Communication on applying the global approach to migration to the Eastern and South-Eastern regions neighbouring the European Union, COM(2007) 247 final, 16.05.2007; EC Communication on towards a common immigration policy, COM(2007) 780 final, 05.12.2007.

11. EC Communication on circular migration and mobility partnerships between the EU and third countries, COM(2007) 248 final, 16.05.2007. In this context three recently adopted directives should also be mentioned (Directive 2003/109/EC on the status of long-term residents; Directive 2004/114/EC on the admission of third-country nationals for the purposes of studies, pupil exchanges, unremunerated training or voluntary services; and Directive 2005/71/EC on the admission of researchers).

12. Proposal for a Directive on the admission of highly skilled migrants—"EU Blue Card," Proposal for a Directive on the admission of seasonal migrants, and Proposal for a Directive on the admission of remunerated trainees.

13. http://www.workpermit.com/news/2007-10-23/europe/european-union-blue-card-scheme-unveiled-in-strasbourg-franco-frattini.htm

14. Green Paper on an EU approach to managing economic migration, COM(2004) 811 final, 11.01.2005, and EC Communication on policy plan on legal migration, SEC(2005)1680, COM(2005) 669 final, 21.12.2005.

15. Commission Staff Working Document: Impact Assessment on a common immigration policy for Europe: principles, actions and tools, SEC(2008) 2026, 17.06.2008; and summary of the impact assessment SEC(2008) 2027. http://www.europarl.europa.eu/registre/docs_autres_institutions/commission_europeenne/sec/2008/2027/COM_SEC(2008)2027_EN.pdf

16. EC Green Paper on migration and mobility: challenges and opportunities for EU education systems, SEC(2008)2173 and COM(2008) 423 final, 3.7.2008. http://ec.europa.eu/education/school21/sec2173_en.pdf

17. COM(2005) 389 final. http://eur-lex.europa.eu/LexUriServ/LexUriServ.do?uri=COM:2005:0389:FIN:EN:PDF

18. Council Document 14615/04. http://eur-lex.europa.eu/LexUriServ/LexUriServ.do?uri=COM:2005:0669:FIN:IT:HTML

19. In particular, in "emergency situations" or when an "exceptionally large number" of transition and developing-country nationals places "an unforeseen heavy burden" on the administrative or judicial capacity of a member state, that state may decide to allow longer periods for judicial review, as well as less favorable conditions of detention.

20. See the Joint Declaration on a Mobility Partnership between the EU and Moldova and Action Fiche, 05.06.2008. Among the proposed activities, the ETF is involved in the monitoring of migration flows through the provision of a methodological tool for analyzing the skills levels of potential and returning migrants in the Moldova Migration Profile, and in contributing to the policy debate on qualification recognition issues and labor-market matching through the promotion of bilateral recognition of skills and qualifications.

21. For the purpose of this report, the following definitions are used: "education" means achievements accomplished at formal education institutions, and "skills" refers to learning outcomes acquired in either formal or informal environments.

22. Government of Albania, *National Strategy on Migration*, Albanian government in cooperation with the International Organization for Migration, Tirana, 2004.

23. Global Migrant Origin Database: http://www.migrationdrc.org/research/typesofmigration/global_migrant_origin_database.html

24. For broader comments on migration dynamics in Eastern Europe and Central Asia, see Mansoor and Quillin (2007).

25. The study was designed by an ETF team of experts, based on the objectives; its survey methodology and sampling technique were developed by Professor Richard Black, University of Sussex, Brighton.

26. For example, of the 90 papers presented at the Third IZA-World Bank Conference held in Rabat May 5–6, 2008, only eight directly concerned skills and human capital. At previous conferences there were even fewer. An exception to this trend is provided by Bardak (2006, 2007).

27. Country reports. http://www.etf.europa.eu

28. When only a returning migrant was present in the household, the interviewer was able to interview him or her as both a returning migrant and a potential migrant.

29. Being conscious that the "snowball" technique is not probabilistic, it was considered the best solution to identify returning migrants during the fieldwork.

CHAPTER 2

Main Results of Data Analysis from the Surveys

The findings below are based on the data from the ETF's potential and returning migrants surveys in four countries. They include an analysis of migration trends, intentions to migrate, factors influencing migration, reasons to migrate, destination choices, actual migration experiences of those who return, the impact of migration on development through remittances, reintegration in the labor market of returning migrants, and entrepreneurship, as well as the factors influencing these outcomes in the four countries: Albania, Egypt, Moldova, and Tunisia.

Migration Trends

The following section focuses on the findings of the potential migrants' surveys, mainly on their intentions to migrate, factors influencing their migration, reasons to migrate and destination choices.

Intentions to Migrate

Notwithstanding the reservations mentioned above concerning individuals' responses and the representativeness of the ETF survey, this research sought to assess the potential for future migration, particularly among the 18–40 age group, where international migration is typically concentrated.

The simple data analysis presented in figure 2.1 shows that 40 percent or more of respondents in all four countries said they were "seriously considering" moving abroad to live and work, with those in Tunisia particularly likely to express an interest in migration. However, less than 20 percent felt that this was likely to be during the next six months, with similar results in all four countries on this measure.

Interestingly, in all four countries the 18- to 40-year-olds interviewed who had already lived and worked abroad were more likely than those who had never been abroad to say that they expected to move abroad again within the next six months (figure 2.2). This is not surprising, since those who have already been abroad will be more confident about going abroad again, their experience having given them a certain know-how (including knowledge of such matters as how to reach the destination country and how to find a job there). Moreover, they might be expected to have already established networks that will facilitate their migration.[1] However, it also demonstrates that having been able to work abroad already is not in itself sufficient to satisfy the demand among 18- to 40-year-olds for such work. The figures also suggest that circular migration will develop as a significant phenomenon, particularly in Albania and Moldova, where the majority of returnees interviewed were under 40, and about half said they were seriously considering going abroad again, mostly within the next two years.

The fact that respondents declare an intention to migrate does not necessarily mean that leaving the country is a real possibility for them.

Figure 2.1   Potential Migrants: Intention to Migrate and Likelihood of Migration (%)

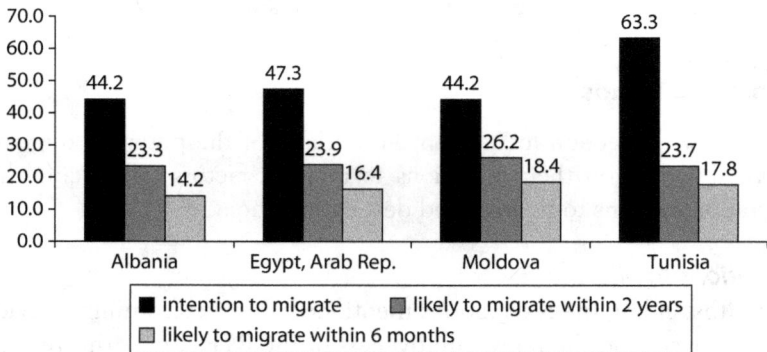

Source: ETF survey data.

Note: This figure is based on the answers to three different questions (see annex 3), as percentages of total respondents. N = 1,001 respondents for Albania, 812 for Egypt, 1,010 for Moldova, and 1,015 for Tunisia.

Figure 2.2   Returning Migrants (18 to 40 Years Old): Intention to Migrate and Likelihood of Migration (%)

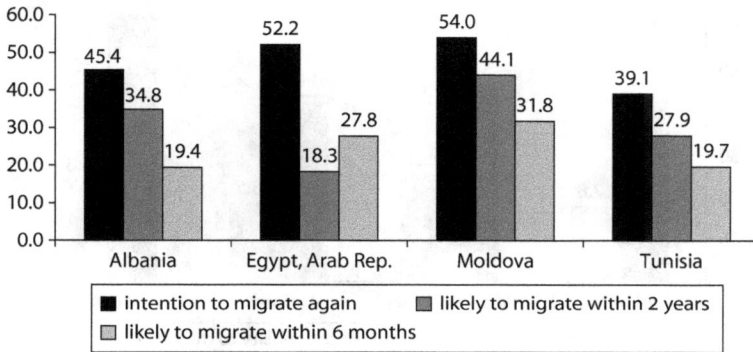

Source: ETF survey data.
Note: This figure is based on the answers to three different questions (see annex 3), as percentages of total respondents. N = 826 respondents for Albania, 230 for Egypt, 689 for Moldova, and 506 for Tunisia.

In order to do so, potential migrants need, among other things, money, documents, language skills, and information. For this reason, in order to understand the real likelihood of migration, a composite variable called "propensity to migrate" has been created for simple data analysis based on the following variables:

- likelihood of migration within six months and within two years
- ability to finance the move
- knowledge of the language of the most likely destination
- information about the most likely destination
- possession of least four of the six necessary documents (such as passport, visa, health certificate, work contract) and no difficulties obtaining the remaining ones

Those who meet at least four of these conditions are considered to be "likely to migrate." Figure 2.3 shows this propensity to migrate of potential migrants in the four countries surveyed. It is clear that percentages decrease strongly when factors other than the declared intention to migrate are taken into account.

In general, the majority of those who were seriously considering a move abroad already had a passport (except in Egypt), enough money to travel (except in Moldova), and what they considered to be sufficient information about the country to which they wished to go. With the

Figure 2.3   Potential Migrants: Intention and Propensity to Migrate (%)

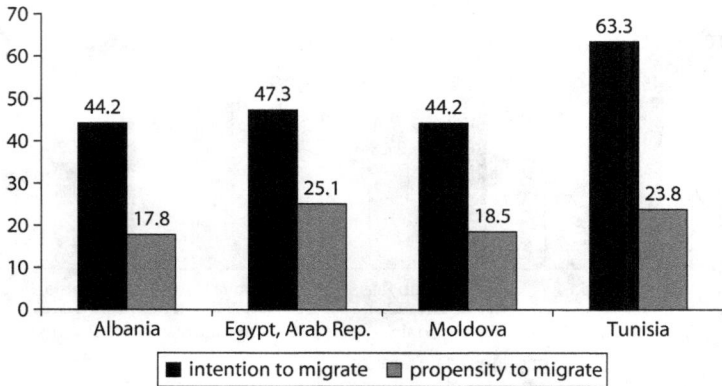

Source: ETF survey data.
Note: This figure is based on the answers to three different questions (see annex 3), as percentages of total respondents. N = 1,001 respondents for Albania, 812 for Egypt, 1,010 for Moldova, and 1,015 for Tunisia.

exception of Albanians, there was also a good level of language competence among these potential migrants, though this partly reflects the fact that many Tunisians planned to go to France, Moldovans to Russia, and Egyptians to the Gulf, where language would not necessarily be an issue. However, in general, very few possessed a work contract, visa, health certificate, or proof of the training or studies they had already completed, and, except in Egypt, most potential migrants felt they would have problems obtaining the documents necessary to leave their country (see annex 2, table A2).

Once again, some caution is required in the interpretation of these figures. For example, rightly or wrongly, the majority of those interviewed did not regard a health certificate, proof of education, or indeed a work contract as something they needed in order to be able to migrate. In this context it is the lack of a visa for travel that stands out as the major impediment to migration, with fewer than 10 percent of potential migrants in any of the countries in the study already having one. It is worth noting here that few potential migrants either knew about, or intended to participate in, government schemes to facilitate migration, and few return migrants had used them when they first migrated.

Socioeconomic Factors Influencing Migration
Age, gender, and marital status. Simple data analysis on potential migrants suggests that younger single males without children are most likely to

migrate, a finding that is in line with most migration studies. Overall, it is likely to be the children rather than the heads of households who intend to move. Moldova is the exception to this trend, as both heads of households and their sons or daughters are the most likely to have intentions to migrate.

Education. The main concern of this study is the way in which migration interacts with education and training. According to the literature, migrants tend to be relatively well educated, compared to the population as a whole, in source countries (te Velde 2005). For example, data compiled by researchers for the World Bank suggest that skilled individuals (those with tertiary education) are twice as likely to migrate as the population as a whole in Central and Eastern European transition countries, and three times as likely in the Middle East and North Africa (Docquier and Marfouk 2006).

Descriptive data analysis of the survey does not entirely confirm this trend. Among those who have not yet migrated, there is no significant link between the level of education and the wish to migrate, except in Egypt. This means that in the data, intentions to migrate do not vary with the level of education or, in other words, respondents with different educational levels present similar percentages in terms of their intention to migrate. The exception, in line with the literature, is Egypt, where the higher the level of education, the higher the percentage of those who wish to migrate. This fact may be linked with the job opportunities for highly educated people in those Gulf countries that are the main destinations for Egyptians.

Among returning migrants there is a statistically significant relationship between the educational level and the intention to re-emigrate in Albania, Egypt, and Tunisia. However, this correlation is relatively strong only in Albania, where the lower the educational level of returning migrants, the higher the intention to migrate again. This is a result of both internal and external factors. First, individuals with low and medium levels of education have more difficulty finding a job in Albania,[2] while there are more opportunities for those with higher skills levels and overseas experience to integrate into the domestic labor market. Second, and more important, migration for respondents with the lowest levels of education failed more often, in the sense that they were sent away by authorities or that their permits abroad expired.[3] This failure becomes a push factor for remigration,[4] which is reinforced by the greater availability of unskilled jobs in the main destination countries of Albanian migrants.

In Albania and Tunisia, the field of study has an impact on the intention to migrate. The tendency to migrate is higher in Albania for those who have studied education and agriculture, and in Tunisia for those who have studied humanities, arts, and sciences. This potentially reflects the demands of the labor markets in these countries.

The main reasons for migrating were, not surprisingly, a desire to improve standards of living, and a response to unemployment. "To study" was mentioned as the main reason for migrating by, on average, only 4 percent of potential migrants, and "to finance children's education" by an additional 1.5 percent. The highest percentages of those intending to migrate to study were for Albania and Tunisia (5.4 percent and 5.5 percent, respectively). Very few[5] returning migrants who were planning to go abroad again said that this was to further their education. Interestingly, most of the (few) returning migrants who migrated to study followed university courses while they were abroad, except Moldovans, but this information cannot be generalized because of the low response rate.

Language skills. Language skills appeared to be a significant factor in the migration decision only in Moldova and Tunisia, where those who knew at least one foreign language were more likely to migrate than those who know only their native tongue. This is because the proportion of people speaking languages other than their native tongue is relatively large in the sample: Many Tunisians speak French, many Albanians speak Italian and some Greek, and a large number of Moldavians speak Russian. Such language skills are in line with the common destinations of migrants from the respective countries, but are not necessarily limited to those who want to migrate. A more detailed analysis on the impact of language skills on intentions to migrate is presented later in this section of the study.

Labor-market status. The simple data analysis reveals that, overall, unemployed people are most likely to intend to migrate, followed by casual workers and students. The details by country are shown in table 2.1.

Overall, the construction, transport, and hospitality sectors are those in which more individuals intended to migrate. The trends were similar in all four countries, with the addition of the domestic sector in Albania, and especially Moldova, and of the maintenance sector in Egypt and Tunisia.[6]

Not surprisingly, unskilled and skilled workers are generally more likely to migrate than professionals or managers.[7] Nevertheless, the percentages of professionals and managers who said they were seriously thinking of leaving their country were above 30 percent in all four countries, with the

Table 2.1   Labor-Market Status by Country and Intention to Migrate

	Albania		Egypt, Arab Rep.		Moldova		Tunisia		Total (N)	
	Stay (%)	Move (%)	Stay (%)	Move (%)	Stay (%)	Move (%)	Stay (%)	Move (%)	Stay	Move
Employed	55.1	44.9	59.4	40.6	59.1	40.9	44.4	55.6	747	615
Employer	70.2	29.8	57.1	42.9	59.7	40.3	54.4	45.6	351	212
Casual worker	31.6	68.4	42.1	57.9	52.8	47.2	25.4	74.6	170	244
Student	66.7	33.3	53.4	46.6	50.0	50.0	29.8	70.2	273	308
Unemployed	36.5	63.5	43.2	56.8	51.8	48.2	18.8	81.2	255	417
Never worked and unknown	51.4	48.6	0.0	0.0	60.0	40.0	63.0	37.0	118	86
Total (N)	558	440	428	384	563	446	365	612	1914	1882

Source: ETF survey data.

highest rates in Tunisia (41 percent and 54 percent of professionals and high managers, respectively, said they intended to migrate).

This indicates that the fact of being employed does not prevent migration. Although unemployed people are more likely to consider migration, people who are employed, even in theoretically good posts (such as employers, managers, and professionals), also demonstrate high levels of intention to migrate. It appears that decent jobs, with good salaries and conditions, are essential for reducing the intention to migrate.

Sources of income: remittances. The surveys provided information on several income sources of respondents:[8] Income from other family members, rent, savings, pensions and social assistance, land, and income from remittances. Individuals also stated whether or not they considered their income to be sufficient.

Figure 2.4 shows that those who receive remittances were more likely to consider migration.[9] This general trend is not surprising, since respondents who receive remittances are more exposed to the idea of migrating and already part of a network that may facilitate migration. This variable is also used in the econometric analysis and distinguishes between individuals who regularly receive remittances and those who receive remittances only sometimes.

Reasons for Migrating

Traditional economic theory identifies universal wage differentials between labor-exporting and labor-receiving countries as the main reason for migration, particularly for qualified workers. Additionally, for rural

Figure 2.4   Remittances and Intention to Migrate (%)

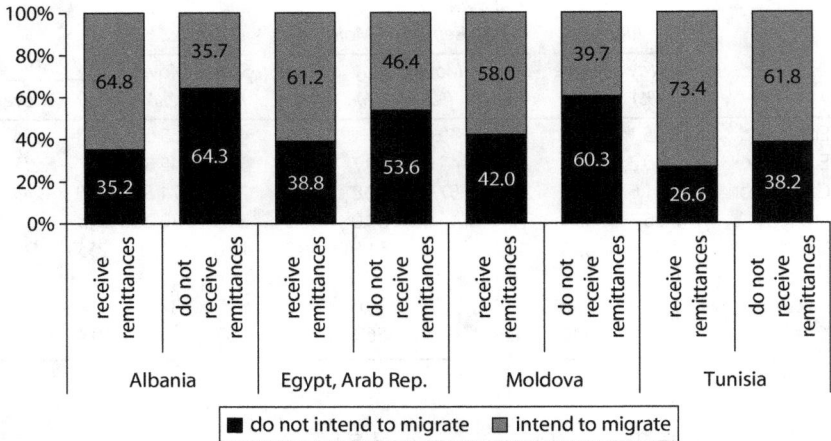

Source: ETF survey data.
Note: N = 998 respondents in Albania, 812 in Egypt, 1,009 in Moldova, and 987 in Tunisia.

families migration is said to represent a form of self-insurance that is used as one of several strategies for economic survival. This is confirmed by a study carried out by MIREM (Collective Action to Support the Reintegration of Return Migrants in their Country of Origin project) on returnees, despite its relatively small sample. According to this study, migration from the Maghreb (Algeria, Morocco, and Tunisia) is motivated mainly by economic or job-related reasons, with sharp differences between men and women, with half of all female migrants moving for reasons of family reunification (Gubert and Norman 2008).

The "relative deprivation" theory, on the other hand, was developed through consideration of well-situated professionals at home and similarly trained professionals abroad. In the first group, people acquire their careers in relatively good conditions and lead a middle-class existence in their own country. The inability to meet this standard is a powerful motivator for departure. In other words, it is not the comparison of salaries with those paid in the developed world that becomes the key determinant of brain drain, but the inability to access remuneration that makes a decent lifestyle possible in their own country, and particularly in their local community (Stark and Taylor 1991). The central source of relative deprivation is not salary differentials, but working conditions and opportunities for self-development (Castles and Delgado Wise 2008). In fact, Boubakri (2004) and Baldwin-Edwards (2005) show that very high unemployment among university graduates and a general lack of career opportunities and job satisfaction in the Maghreb are the main reasons for the increasing migration of higher-skilled individuals.

Finally, the migration transition theory is the notion that societies and countries, in parallel with economic restructuring and concomitant social change and demographic transition, tend to go through a sequence in relation to migration. This is characterized by initially increasing outward migration, followed by the coexistence of significant but diminishing outward migration and increasing inward migration; this eventually creates net immigration countries (Skeldon 1997).[10] This is linked to the notion of a "migration hump," developed by Martin and Taylor (1996), who argue that a temporary increase in migration—the hump—has been a usual part of the process of economic development, since a certain threshold of wealth is necessary to enable people to assume the costs and risks of migrating.

Increasing incomes, the development of transport and communication infrastructures, improved access to education and information, and the concomitant process of social and cultural change are factors that tend to give people the abilities and aspirations to migrate, which they first tend to do for the most part internally, then, in later stages, increasingly internationally. Only in the longer term does outward migration tend to decrease and do countries tend to change from net-emigration to net-immigration countries. In the 19th and 20th centuries, most Western European countries went through such a migration transition process. In recent decades, countries such as Spain, Italy, Greece, and Ireland in Europe and Malaysia, Taiwan, and South Korea in Asia have completed their migration transition. On the basis of persistent expansion of the greater European migration system, the challenging question is whether or not North Africa and Eastern Europe will also go through similar migration transitions, and whether this will occur in the near future.

When potential migrants were asked why they were considering migrating abroad, explanations linked to (un)employment and poverty featured prominently. More than 50 percent of potential migrants, regardless of the country, mentioned that their reason for leaving was "to improve [their] standard of living" or because they had no job. Egyptians were about twice as likely as respondents in the other three countries to report that they would move because they had no job. This is in line with both wage differential and "relative deprivation" theories. In particular, the finding about the high levels of managers and professionals intending to emigrate to look for decent jobs, salaries, and conditions confirms the relative deprivation theory.

A lower percentage of people said that they would migrate because their current work was unsatisfactory (ranging from 1.6 percent in Egypt to 9.3 percent in Albania) or because they wanted a higher salary (0 percent in Albania, but 9.4 percent in Moldova, as shown in table 2.2).[11] Indeed, an average of 7.3 percent (with national values ranging from 2.9 percent in Albania to 10.7 percent in Egypt) responded strongly that "there is no future here," which may indicate an extremely hopeless situation (economically, socially, or politically).

A small number of people—7.5 percent overall—cited family factors as the main reason why they would move. This was notably the case in Albania, where more than 10 percent said they would move to follow a spouse or parent, and in Egypt, where just under 10 percent said they

Table 2.2   Main Motivation for Leaving among Potential Migrants, by Country

Motivation for leaving	Albania (%)	Egypt, Arab Rep. (%)	Moldova (%)	Tunisia (%)	Total (%)
Economic	65.8	73.7	73.7	64.4	68.8
To improve standard of living	36.7	23.7	38.2	40.1	35.5
Have no job/cannot find a job	19.7	40.9	14.4	13.2	20.6
Nature of work unsatisfactory	9.3	1.6	8.1	3.5	5.5
To earn higher salary	0.0	6.8	9.4	5.4	5.4
To repay debts	0.2	0.8	2.5	1.9	1.4
Inadequate social security system	0.0	0.0	1.1	0.3	0.4
Education	8.1	1.3	6.5	5.5	5.5
To obtain education	5.4	0.8	3.1	5.5	4.0
To finance children's education	2.7	0.5	3.4	0.0	1.5
Family	11.1	10.4	3.1	6.2	7.5
To accompany/follow spouse/parent	10.2	1.3	1.8	1.9	3.7
To get married/just married	0.5	8.9	0.7	3.2	3.1
To escape from family problems	0.5	0.3	0.7	1.1	0.7
Other	14.9	14.6	16.4	23.8	18.2
No future here	2.9	10.7	8.5	7.6	7.3
Want to go abroad	2.7	0.5	2.9	5.8	3.4
Do not like living in this country	2.3	0.5	1.1	6.6	3.1
Adventure	0.2	0.5	0.2	3.0	1.2
To receive necessary health care	1.1	0.0	0.2	0.2	0.4
Other	5.7	2.3	3.4	0.6	2.8
Don't know	0.0	0.0	0.2	0.2	0.1
N=	442	384	445	634	1,905

Source: ETF survey data.

would move in order to get married.[12] There were also a number of "other" reasons, most commonly expressed as "no future here," "want to live abroad," or "do not like living in this country."

These results must be interpreted with caution, since people may have multiple reasons for thinking about (or rejecting) migration,[13] and because they may not wish to admit, or may not even be aware of, the real reason that they are considering migrating. Economic factors are clearly important overall, outweighing as they do all other factors put together. Nonetheless, the role of education and work experience in influencing some aspects of migration, notably the destination to which people aspire to go and the kind of work they wish to do, does emerge from the survey. These aspirations are explored in the following section.

Findings of the Econometric Analysis: Intentions to Migrate and Their Realization

The previous trends can be checked and synthesized through a (multivariable) econometric analysis. This analysis uses two different models to determine the migration intentions: a logit and an ordered logit model. The first model includes variables that resulted from questions that were asked of all the individuals interviewed, and therefore includes the whole sample. The dependent variable, like the descriptive analysis, is based on whether an individual intended to move. The second model analyzes only those intending to move, and allows various variables that are only available to be added to this subsample. The dependent variable is ordered and distinguishes between different levels of likelihood that individuals will actually realize their intentions. The three categories—maybe, likely, and certain—are calculated based on the set of variables previously mentioned in the descriptive analysis.[14] Although it is possible to distinguish between gradually increasing likelihoods of migration, it should be kept in mind that there is no observation of who will actually migrate, only of people's intentions. As it is quite clear that the four countries all have their own characteristics that contribute to the migration intentions of their people, all models include country dummies to control for these country-specific characteristics. This section will concentrate on the main results only.[15]

Both models show that, after controlling for other relevant factors, age appears to have no effect on the likelihood of being a potential migrant or of realizing migration intentions. While this finding contradicts previous literature, it is likely to be caused simply by the age restriction within the sample (18–40 years).[16]

Women appear to be less likely to move. The marginal effects show a significant decrease of 23 percent in the likelihood of migration intentions. In addition, the proportional odds in the second model decrease by 24 percent, indicating that women are also less sure about their intentions. Furthermore, the number of children in a household has a negative impact on the intention to migrate—the odds ratio is 0.81. Moreover, the head of household is the least likely to intend to migrate, and marital status is insignificant in the first model. In the second model, however, marital status is significant. Married people appear to be more certain than single people about realizing their migration intentions. This may reflect the fact that they also have to take responsibility for family members and might therefore have given more thought to the practical issues of migration.

The ability to speak at least one language in addition to the native tongue is significantly and positively associated with the intention to migrate. The marginal effect is 10 percent. This seems to contradict what was said in the descriptive analysis (where as described, languages were relevant in Moldova and Tunisia only). Simple cross-tables presented are hiding effects from other variables. The estimations done in this econometrical analysis show that speaking at least one foreign language is relevant for Moldova and even more so for Albania. These two countries influence the whole sample.

Moreover, the second model allows specific language skills to be controlled for—that is, whether individuals speak the language of the country to which they wish to move. A reasonable ability to speak these languages does not significantly influence the realization of intentions, but not being able to speak the relevant language constitutes a significant obstacle. This finding confirms those of other studies on the role of language skills in migration.[17]

Both models reveal interesting results regarding education. Higher levels of education are significantly positive, compared to low education levels (medium levels are insignificant) in both models. However, these results hide country-specific differences. Analysis by country shows that the result is mainly driven by Egypt. This may be because of the particular characteristics of Egyptian migration. The main destination area for Egyptians is Saudi Arabia and other Gulf countries, through a well-regulated migration process managed by private recruitment companies, and the primary demand is for highly educated workers. Thus, migration is more of an option for skilled rather than low-skilled workers, with skilled individuals also on average being more able to finance migration.

In order to understand the effect of education across countries better, education and country dummies were interacted. This allowed a specific examination of the problem that the findings on education may be driven by the sample from Egypt, while simultaneously keeping the larger sample size, which would be lost in a country-level analysis. The results show that higher levels of education are now insignificant. Since Albania is the base outcome for the countries, this concerns highly educated Albanians. Country dummy estimates are negative and significant for Egypt and Moldova, and positive and significant for Tunisia. As expected, the interaction effect of Egypt with tertiary education is large, positive, and significant. Interaction effects of secondary education are significant and positive in the basic model for Egypt and, in a more intense way, Moldova. This means that Egypt is in fact driving the positive effect of higher education, while education is less relevant for Albania and irrelevant for Tunisia and Moldova. For more details on the econometric analysis, see Avato (2009).

Notes

1. The existence of networks is a very important factor in facilitating migration. They provide information about the country, job opportunities, and even direct assistance to the migrant. This is confirmed by the fact that having friends or relatives in the country is the main reason for preferring a particular destination country for potential migrants in Albania (35.4 percent), the second in Egypt (20.8 percent), and the third in Moldova and Tunisia (14.4 percent and 11.4 percent, respectively). See also Palloni et al. (2001).

2. An examination of unemployment rates by level of education reveals that this is also true in Moldova and Tunisia.

3. Survey data show that this trend is true, except in Egypt.

4. This trend is also proved by the survey data. It is particularly marked in Albania.

5. A total of only eight individuals, across all four countries. This is not really surprising, because returning migrants are already involved in the labor market and generally consider that the time for studying has passed. Nevertheless, 7 percent of returning migrants who intended to re-emigrate from Moldova said they wished to do this in order to finance their children's education.

6. In addition, 75 percent of information and communication technology workers in Tunisia said they were seriously thinking of leaving their country, though there were only 16 respondents working in this sector. Thus, this information cannot be generalized.

7. Migrants were asked about the level of skills and responsibilities required by their job. They could choose between "high management," "middle management,"

"professional," "skilled worker," "'unskilled worker," and "other." Respondents were asked to choose the category that best fitted their case. In terms of skills match, highly educated respondents would be expected to be in the managerial or professional categories, workers with VET qualifications would at least be in "skilled workers," and those without any qualifications in "unskilled workers."

8. In euros and adjusted by 2006 exchange rates.

9. In Tunisia this link is not statistically significant.

10. This is currently the case of countries like Ukraine (ETF 2008, 2009), as well as EU member states such as Poland and Romania.

11. Interestingly, in all four countries analyzed, managers considering migration were the most inclined to explain that their main reason was to look for higher salaries.

12. It is likely that the majority selecting this response in Egypt were going abroad to earn enough money to get married, rather than going to get married abroad.

13. Respondents were asked to give three reasons for migrating and to identify their main reason.

14. For example, respondents were asked how likely it is that they will move within the next six months or within the next two years; about their ability to finance migration; and various questions about whether they know about, and already possess, certain prerequisites such as passport, visa, work contract, or approval for study. Including these variables, the ordered dependent variable is calculated based on (1) the individual perception of how likely migration is within a certain time and (2) factors that constitute a constraint to migration, such as immigration policy and financial constraints.

15. More detailed result tables can be obtained from the ETF.

16. Other specifications like adding a squared age term were tried but did not show any effect.

17. See, for example, Chiswick (2000).

CHAPTER 3

Migration Policy and Its Skill Dimensions

The four countries analyzed here have different migration histories; thus their migration policies and interaction with migrants and host countries are different. This is also reflected in the different types of agreements (whose effectiveness is in question) that they signed with different host countries. A migration project is still an individual project that largely follows market incentives through irregular channels. This partly explains the common skills mismatch of migrants in the host countries. Employing tools such as qualification recognition, among other actions, could help to capitalize migrants' skills, enhancing the benefits for the host country, the sending country, and the migrant himself. Therefore the skills dimension of migrants needs to be taken into account in the migration policies of both sending and receiving countries.

Migration Policies of the Four Home Countries

All four countries in this study have initiated reasonably comprehensive policies toward migration, with all except Tunisia having a basic law covering emigration issues, and all having either a ministry or an executive agency with overall responsibility for emigration (table 3.1). It is also important to recall that a long tradition of emigration in the cases of Egypt and Tunisia helped these countries develop more tools and policies,

Table 3.1   Legislative Arrangements on Emigration Policy

Country	Basic law on emigration	Date	Ministry or agency responsible
Albania	Law No. 9668 on the Emigration of Albanian Citizens for Reasons of Employment	2006	Ministry of Labor, Social Affairs and Equal Opportunities Inter-Ministerial Committee on Migration
Egypt, Arab Rep.	Law No. 111 on Emigration and Sponsoring Egyptians Abroad	1983	Ministry of Manpower and Emigration Higher Committee for Migration
Moldova	Law No. 1518-XV on Migration	2002	Ministry of Economy and Trade (National Migration Bureau—closed in 2006)
Tunisia	(No basic law on emigration)	n/a	Ministry of Social Affairs and Tunisians Living Abroad Office of Tunisians Abroad

Source: http://www.ilo.org/dyn/natlex/natlex_browse.home?p_lang=en

compared to Albania and Moldova, which have only recent emigration history. In the cases of Egypt and Tunisia, the broad framework of emigration policy dates back over two decades to a time when it was viewed in a much more positive light as contributing to labor-market equilibrium, with controlled emigration as an active employment policy instrument.[1] Since that time, the attitude of both these countries has shifted, with consequent uncertainty as to the extent to which legal arrangements and interventionist policies have actually been implemented. Meanwhile, in Albania and Moldova there is also policy uncertainty, though this reflects the reverse position: emigration policies are arguably too recent to have been fully implemented in practice.

Over the past decade, the governments of home countries have placed particular emphasis on facilitating links with their diasporas. The idea behind these policies has been to encourage local development by attracting human, social, and financial capital that has been acquired abroad. In some cases, home countries have also changed their citizenship laws to permit dual nationality and voting rights.[2]

The most wide-reaching and well-established policy on migration is in Tunisia, where despite the lack of basic law on emigration, the government actively seeks to foster a sense of belonging to Tunisia among expatriates, provides services to those living abroad, and encourages the mobilization of skills for development within the country (table 3.2).

Table 3.2   Key Policy Interventions on Emigration

Country	Ministry/Agency	Activity
Albania	Inter-Ministerial Committee on Migration	• Formulation of National Strategy for Migration Management
	Ministry of Labor, Social Affairs and Equal Opportunities	• Emigration Unit drafting plan on use of remittances
	Ministry of Foreign Affairs	• Institute for diaspora—role unclear at present
		• Provision of consular services
		• Negotiation of bilateral agreements
Egypt, Arab Rep.	Ministry of Manpower and Emigration	• Database of expatriate skills
		• Support to "Union of Egyptians Abroad"
		• Development of Integrated Migration Information System (IMIS)
		• Project on Information Dissemination for the Prevention of Irregular Migration from Egypt (IDOM)
		• Negotiated labor agreement with Italy (2004)
	Higher Committee for Migration	• Runs 23 professional training centers and specialized courses for predeparture training
		• Provides services and facilities for emigrants
	Ministry of Foreign Affairs	• Provides consular services for emigrants
Moldova	Ministry of Economy and Trade	• Development of policy on employment abroad
		• Support to expatriates
		• Runs program targeting uses of remittances for business promotion
	National Employment Agency	• Planned responsibility for placing Moldovan workers abroad
Tunisia	Ministry of Foreign Affairs/OTE	• Provides range of support services to expatriates
		• Runs 16 *"Espaces femmes et 2ème génération"*
	Caisse Nationale de Securité Sociale	• Manages pension funds of expatriates
		• Negotiates bilateral agreements on social protection of Tunisian workers
	Ministry of Work	• Negotiates bilateral labor agreements
		• Facilitates reinsertion of returnees
	Agence Tunisienne de Coopération Technique (ATCT)	• Maintains database of Tunisian skilled individuals
		• Promotes placement of skilled Tunisians abroad
	APIA/API/APIE	• Run dedicated bureaus for expatriate investment in Tunisia

Source: ETF country migration profiles.[3]

Tunisia has bilateral social security agreements with at least nine countries to facilitate the flow of social welfare benefits and pensions,[4] and it cooperates with two Italian-funded migration and development programs, one of which focuses on the training of potential migrants. Tunisia also actively seeks to place skilled and unskilled workers abroad, although currently some 80 percent of skilled Tunisians go to Gulf countries. Discussions with Italy are ongoing about the possibility of a bilateral arrangement for skilled migration, but otherwise Tunisia's cooperation with European initiatives is focused more on preventing illegal migration and improving border management.

Egypt also has a long-running policy of promoting international migration, with the Gulf States (table 3.3), and through the annual quota system agreement with Italy.[5] In principle, the Egyptian Ministry for Manpower and Emigration mirrors the work of similar institutions in Tunisia, although there is less emphasis on reaching out and providing services to Egyptians living abroad. Egypt cooperates with two Italian-funded projects to match Egyptian workers with potential jobs abroad, to provide a "portal" of employment opportunities for those who wish to migrate (IMIS[6]) and to discourage irregular migration (IDOM[7]). However, there is still a need for further capacity building.

In Albania and Moldova, a strategic approach to migration has only very recently been taken. In Albania, a comprehensive migration strategy and action plan, financed by the EU, was agreed to in 2005. It includes an attempt to reach out to Albanians living abroad, but it has not yet been substantially implemented. Also in 2005, Albania signed an agreement with the European Union on the readmission of people residing there without authorization. Albania has bilateral labor migration agreements with Italy, Greece, and Germany.

In Moldova, an action plan on migration and asylum was only agreed to in 2006, and arguably even this was called into question by the closure of the Migration Bureau in the same year. Furthermore, although Moldova appears to have more bilateral migration agreements in force than any of the other countries in this report, it is unclear whether these agreements are operational.

On June 5, 2008, Moldova became the first country to sign a mobility partnership with the EU;[8] this is a single framework for joint management of migration flows. The main aim is "to make better use of migration to promote development . . . including bilateral initiatives that encourage the transfer of social security benefits and programs for sustainable reintegration, exchanges, training and temporary work."

Table 3.3 Signed Bilateral Labor Agreements

Country	Destination	Description	Entered into force	Quota	Current status
Albania	Greece	Mobility of workers	1997	No	Lapsed
	Italy	Mobility of workers	1996	4,500 (2007)	Active
	Germany	Vocational training and youth employment	1991	No	Lapsed
Egypt, Arab Rep.	Sudan	Exchange of workers	2003		Active
	Libya	Mobility of teachers	2003		No information
	Italy	Mobility of workers, including agricultural workers	2001	7,000 (2007)	Active
	Kuwait	Technical cooperation agreement on workforce transference	2001		Active
	Lebanon	Mobility of construction workers	1994		No information
	Sudan	Exchange of workers	2003		Active
	Jordan	Memorandum of Understanding on the Migration of Egyptian Laborers	2007		Active
Moldova	Azerbaijan	Mobility of workers and social protection	2005	No	No information
	Greece	Mobility of workers	2004	No	No information
	Korea	Mobility of workers and social protection	2004	No	No information
	Italy	Mobility of workers	2003	2,500 (2006)	No information
	Ukraine	Labor cooperation	1994		No information
	Belarus	Labor cooperation	1994		No information
	Russia	Labor cooperation	1993		No information
Tunisia	Italy	Mobility of workers	2000	Yes	Active
	France	Mobility of workers	2000	No	Active
	Germany	Recruitment of workers	1965		Ended

Source: Compiled from interviews with public institutions in the four countries, plus Collyer 2004.

In the case of Egypt and Tunisia, official interest has been expressed in promoting the temporary mobility of both skilled and unskilled workers, although in Egypt the major direction of managed migration remains skilled migration to the Gulf rather than to the EU. Meanwhile, there appears to be a gap in all four countries between policies on paper and their implementation in practice.

Overview of Official Emigration Programs and Labor Agreements

Although various programs and agreements exist in the four countries, as outlined above, it is far from clear that such programs are effective. Looking first at departure, only 10 percent of the returning migrants interviewed reported that they knew of the existence of government schemes or programs to support migration, and even fewer— only 5.4 percent—had used them (table 3.4), with the proportion in Albania and Moldova being negligible. A further 3 percent reported that they had traveled abroad with the assistance of a private recruitment company, but even this practice was limited mainly to Egypt and

Table 3.4   Awareness and Use of Government Migration Programs and Recruitment Companies

	Albania	Egypt, Arab Rep.	Moldova	Tunisia
Return migrants	*(%)*	*(%)*	*(%)*	*(%)*
Aware of government migration schemes	1.5	8.5	3.2	22.9
Participated in government migration scheme	0.6	6.2	1.5	13.3
Aware of private recruitment companies	0.9	14.2	8.3	6.1
Used private recruitment company	0.6	5.3	5.4	2.0
N=	*1,000*	*1,000*	*1,010*	*986*
Potential migrants	*(%)*	*(%)*	*(%)*	*(%)*
Aware of government migration schemes	12.6	4.1	9.9	23.7
Likely to participate in government scheme	10.9	3.1	6.7	15.8
Aware of private recruitment companies	6.3	18.2	13.7	21.1
Likely to use private recruitment company	5.0	5.7	7.8	15.2
N=	*442*	*384*	*446*	*633*

Source: ETF survey data.

Moldova, and to destinations outside the EU. The main reasons cited by those who were aware of legal migration schemes or private recruitment companies but did not intend to use them included that they were "too expensive," "not transparent," or not suitable for the individual's level of qualifications.

The lack of use of official programs and agreements is not surprising, given both the limited size of quotas for labor mobility that exist and the way in which programs appear to be implemented in practice. For example, Italy is one of the few European countries to include quotas for legal migration in bilateral labor agreements, but the numbers involved are very small. In addition, it seems likely that many of those who benefit were already living and working in Italy illegally, so the agreements are used mainly for regularization. For instance, in the case of Moldova, quotas for legal migration to Italy were set in 2006 at 5,000 and in 2007 at 6,500, which is about 10 percent of the total estimated number of Moldovan migrants in Italy. Even with the rise of 1,500 more in the new quota from 2006 to 2007, the impact in terms of promoting legal migration would have been minimal, especially taking into account that the estimated number of Moldovans in Italy grew by 700 percent between 2002 and 2007.[9] In contrast, it has proved difficult to fill the quota of 7,000 workers (in 2006) established by the bilateral agreement between Egypt and Italy, with fewer than 1,000 migrating over the past two years, to some extent as a result of a shortage of candidates with appropriate qualifications.

One possible example of good practice in terms of official programs to promote migration and skills match is that of the Agence Tunisienne de Coopération Technique (ATCT), which placed about 2,500 skilled Tunisians in jobs abroad in 2006, from a databank of more than 11,000 skilled individuals.

However, in all four countries there is still a general lack of effective implementation of migration policy that could successfully channel temporary skilled migration to the EU, or exploit such migration to deliver development benefits to the home country. In fact, migration strongly follows market incentives and informal channels. Organized migration that might effectively achieve skills matching in particular is practically nonexistent. The few programs in place are not well known, or if they are known, have a negative image among migrants due to implementation problems. In this context there is a need for better organization of and publicity for migration schemes, including using the channels of organized networks (for example, existing migrant communities).

Overview of Official Return Programs and Experiences Following Return

The return experience also largely follows informal channels. Only a small proportion of the returning migrants interviewed had even heard of the government programs that offered incentives to return, and only 1 percent overall had benefited from such schemes. The highest level of knowledge of return schemes was in Tunisia, reflecting the fact that the Tunisian government has taken specific policy steps to encourage return. However, even there, only 12 percent of the returning migrants interviewed had heard of return programs, and only a quarter of these had actually benefited from these incentives. Elsewhere, the knowledge and use of government return incentives appeared to be negligible.

Despite the lack of knowledge of return programs, the ETF survey findings show that return migration contributes to local development, even to a greater extent than remittances. While savings are more commonly used for productive activities, remittances are mostly used to cover living expenses. Work experience abroad helped some returning migrants to mature and develop a business project: human capital as well as money is required for investment to be made productively. The ETF survey provides little information about the type of businesses created by returning migrants, or about whether these businesses were formal or informal. However, since they are most likely to be family-owned retail enterprises, some of them might be informal.

In order to promote the more productive use of remittances and savings, an efficient business environment is necessary, rather than policy measures specifically directed toward migrants or returnees (Black, King, and Tiemoko 2003). For instance, the low levels of entrepreneurship among returning migrants in Moldova can be partly explained by the discouraging business climate, in particular the policy instability, the legal and administrative burdens, the difficulties in accessing finance, and the high costs of doing business (Munteanu 2001; Rutkowski 2004; Eskola 2007; de Rosa and Uregian 2008).

The fact that those who appeared to have fared better since their return were those who had worked in professional or managerial positions while abroad supports the idea of temporary skilled-labor migration to the EU, but does not reflect the reality in many EU countries. In practice, there is greater concern for enforcing the circular migration of unskilled migrants, and a tacit acceptance that many skilled migrants will remain. In any case, it is clear that successful migrants are those with the highest potential to contribute to the development of their home countries.

The ETF survey provides some discouraging evidence on this issue:

- Returning migrants had spent insufficient time abroad to meet their goals in relation to investment back home.
- Returning migrants to Moldova and Tunisia had problems reintegrating themselves in the labor market.
- In all four countries, returning migrants rarely returned to work at home in the same sector in which they had worked abroad.
- Over half of the returning migrants——and many more than this in Moldova——did not feel that their experiences abroad had helped them since their return.

Evidence shows that there are many issues to be tackled in the countries surveyed, in order to improve government programs to promote return migration and a more productive use of remittances, savings, and skills:

- The fiscal advantages or benefits from savings may be offered to remittance recipients or returnees, to encourage reinvestment.
- Advice and support should be offered to returning migrants who intend to set up a business.
- Entrepreneurship education should be introduced; starting from the early years of schooling. This could contribute to creating a positive environment and imparting basic skills to take advantage of opportunities.
- Access to credit needs to be improved.
- The transfer costs of remittances should be reduced.
- Social security coverage could be extended to migrants. Even if survey data show that social security coverage is not amongst the main preoccupations of migrants, such coverage may incentivize return and provide a sort of "safety net" to returning migrants who intend to take the risk of investing.

A complementary policy approach would be to foster the links between those who are overseas and their home countries by facilitating remittances, investment, knowledge exchange, and other development-related processes. However, it is still a significant policy challenge to steer remittances toward areas in which they will have maximum developmental impact, at the same time recognize that they are private transfers, not a substitute for government or development agency action.

The Skills Dimension of Migration: Match or Mismatch?

The concept of "brain drain" is a complex one. It is defined by the OECD (2007) as a "loss of skills for the source country, loss of ideas and innovation, loss of the nation's investment in education and loss of tax revenues, but most importantly the loss of critical services in the health and education services." It began in the 1970s and was seen mainly as a negative phenomenon for home countries. In the mid-1990s the so-called new economics of brain drain were developed, stating that the benefits of skilled migration can outweigh the costs. The idea behind this concept is that in an economy that is open to migration, there are incentives for the population to pursue a higher level of human capital because of the higher prospects for returns on this in foreign countries; this phenomenon can also increase the overall level of human capital in the domestic economy (Stark 2004).

This theory has been challenged; furthermore, according to the ETF survey results, migration per se was not an incentive for pursuing particular types of studies (0.97 percent). In addition, few potential migrants stated that their main intention in migrating was to study (4 percent), and few returning migrants had plans to invest their resources in education (17.4 percent said education was one of the uses of their remittances, and only 0.4 percent mentioned education as one of the uses of migration savings). Nevertheless, this does not account for the nonformal education that can still be achieved when migrants are abroad to improve their level of human capital. For example, new languages may not be learned through a formal education process, but can still add value to the human capital, as do skills learned during employment, which may be transferred to their home country after return.

The data from the ETF survey on returning migrants show that there are different levels of brain waste in the countries surveyed. In Albania and Moldova, more than 60 percent of the highly educated returning migrants had worked abroad as unskilled labor, while in Tunisia the proportion was 12.5 percent and in Egypt 4.5 percent (see annex 2, table A4). These differences may be explained to a certain extent by the different characteristics of migration from the countries surveyed. Egypt and Tunisia are traditional sources of migration with consolidated diaspora networks that can facilitate the potential access to better-quality jobs.

It is difficult to quantify the extent of brain drain, especially in monetary terms. Its harmful effects are usually classified into three categories:

1. the impact on productivity and governance
2. the loss of potential tax revenues

3. the deterioration of critical social services, in particular health and education (OECD 2007)

Another often-cited negative effect for home countries is the loss of return on investments in education. This raises an interesting aspect of the discussion on brain drain that needs to be further investigated and quantified: the effectiveness and productive use of highly skilled workers in home countries. There is an increased interest in higher education in all countries. There are various reasons for this phenomenon:

• culture and tradition: society considers higher education prestigious
• postponing entry into the labor market because of the difficulties of finding a job
• expectations for a better future
• improved access to and affordability of higher education

These factors are not necessarily linked to current or future labor-market needs. For example, in Moldova there is a high demand for higher education; however, the local labor market cannot absorb all those who achieve this level. In Egypt, the government has, until recently, offered employment almost automatically to all university graduates, regardless of their educational background. This has created an artificial incentive to pursue higher education that does not correspond to the real needs of the economy. Under these conditions the concept of brain drain becomes less relevant, because migration may imply the use abroad of a "surplus" of skilled resources. Possible brain waste abroad remains an issue, as is evident in the cases of Albania and Moldova.

Beside skills mismatch, the issue of brain drain is also linked to the types of jobs that are available locally. The countries in the ETF study present a limited number of opportunities for researchers. According to UNDP (2006), there are 172 researchers and 201 technicians in research and development (R&D) per million inhabitants in Moldova, while the figures in Tunisia are 1,073 and 34, respectively. In countries such as France, Germany, the United States, and even Russia, the number of researchers is more than 3,000 per million inhabitants. For researchers, migration may be an open door to opportunities that the home countries are currently unable to provide.

At the graduate and postgraduate levels, the cost of education is sometimes partly or entirely financed by the host countries. The number of students abroad from the four countries surveyed is growing. In 2006, there were about 7,000 Egyptians studying abroad, 9,000 Moldovans, and more than 16,000 Albanians and a similar number of Tunisians.[10] Here the benefit for home countries might accrue in the future in the form of business investment, technology transfer, and improved commercial networks.

There are differences among the countries included in the ETF study in terms of attitudes toward the export of highly skilled workers. In Tunisia, education policy is directed toward the further expansion of higher education, including for the purpose of sending skilled labor abroad. According to the projections of the Tunisian Ministry of Higher Education, the expected number of graduates from higher education will reach 500,000 in 2010 (Tunisian Ministry of Higher Education 2005). Of course, the risk of such a policy is human-capital waste in both the emigration and the immigration country.

In order to reduce brain drain and to obtain maximum benefit from highly skilled individuals, a combination of policy interventions is necessary, including an education system that is closer to the reality of the labor market. In addition, there should be a coherent policy for economic development, with clear sectoral priorities and allocated resources. This conducive environment should in turn attract additional resources in the form of national and foreign investments, which can also activate the highly skilled diasporas and use them for the benefit of the home countries, leading to "brain circulation." There is currently an emphasis in all four countries on maintaining contact with the expatriate population. However, according to the ETF survey, there are very few schemes to assist returning migrants in settling back home and in capitalizing on their human and financial resources.

The European Union as a Migration Destination

On the basis of extensive data analysis, Fargues (2005) revealed a pattern in which Europe attracts those with lower levels of education, while the United States and Canada succeed in attracting most of the higher-skilled North Africans. The ETF survey findings also confirm that the EU is not the most attractive destination for highly skilled migrants, who generally prefer North America or, in the case of Egyptians, the Gulf countries. Moreover, those returning from the EU were less than half as likely to have higher levels of education as those returning from North America or the Gulf. Within the EU, Greece and Italy were highlighted as particular destinations for low-skilled migration. Only in Moldova was the pattern different. Here, individuals with lower skills levels were more likely to be planning to go to Russia than to the EU. However, even in Moldova there was a significant amount of low-skill migration to Europe. It is important to note that those who were planning to go to the EU had low expectations of being able to use their skills at an appropriate level.

Furthermore, with regard to returning migrants' fields of study, it appears that those coming back from the MENA region—mainly those returning to Egypt, and, to a lesser extent Tunisia, from the Gulf—are most likely to have worked abroad in professions that match their qualification levels and fields. For instance, 60 percent of returning migrants with a background in business administration were working in MENA countries as professionals or managers. However, there are a number of issues concerning this type of scheme. Migration to the Gulf States is based on a sponsorship system called kafala, which provides a legal basis for residency and employment. Migrant workers receive an entry visa and a residence permit only if a Gulf Cooperation Council (GCC)[11] citizen or an institution employs them. Many returning migrants from the EU who had a specific field of study worked in unskilled positions. In no section of the ETF study was there evidence that a significant number of returnees from the EU had been able to exercise their specific professional or technical training. However, an important caveat is that this might simply reflect the fact that skilled migrants to the EU from these countries had not returned, and hence were not included in the sample.[12]

The European Commission has proposed a blue-card scheme to encourage highly skilled immigrants to take jobs in EU economic sectors that are suffering from skill shortages. The scheme was inspired by the U.S. green-card system. The blue card will not replace existing national systems, but will provide an additional channel with a common procedure for legal migration.

The question here is, what kind of skills does Europe need? Prospective analysis on this issue is not conclusive. According to the European Centre for the Development of Vocational Training (CEDEFOP) (2008), there will be a "continuous growth in demand for many high and medium-skilled workers but also for some lower categories." This point of view is not shared by Koettl (2006), who considers that most of the new jobs in Europe will be low-skilled jobs in the services sector.

These differences in results derive from the different methodologies used to make the projections. The econometric model used by CEDEFOP to forecast the needs of the European labor market from the demand side is influenced by the current situation from the supply side. In other words, current mismatches between qualifications and skills needed at work influence the results obtained through the model. Koettl followed a simpler procedure. His model multiplied current levels of labor force participation and education by age group and sex with the demographic projections up to 2050.

Europe's lack of appeal as a destination for highly skilled migrants, combined with skills waste, is a serious issue that policy makers should take into account. According to the ETF survey, the percentage of highly educated respondents who have seriously considered migrating ranged from 38.6 percent in Moldova to 63 percent in Tunisia; about a third of professionals and managers reported that they expected to work at a lower skills level if they migrated to the EU.

Some examples suggest areas in which specific training might be appropriate for preparing workers for the EU labor market, making it possible to achieve a correct match between skills and jobs. In Albania, a private contract between a recruitment agency and specific municipalities in northern Italy had provided mechanisms for the circulation of nurses. Language training and the harmonization of qualifications were provided as part of the package. Demand for nurses from overseas, especially in the eldercare sector, is likely to rise in the EU both for demographic reasons (the aging of the population) and because of the increasing reluctance of the domestic population to work in this sector. Indeed, some countries beyond the "European neighborhood" have already recognized the potential for migration and education linkages in particular areas such as nursing (Aminuzamman 2007),[13] teaching, accountancy, and IT (te Velde 2005; Ruiz 2008).

However, the case of Albanian nurses migrating to Italy also highlights some of the difficulties associated with developing training in home countries that is focused on skills requirements in the EU labor market. For example, it appears that residual problems remain in terms of the recognition of Albanian nursing diplomas in Italy, with significant transaction costs in the case of the example cited above. Even if qualifications are recognized, procedures to validate them are too onerous and make diploma recognition practically impossible. Moreover, even where qualifications are officially recognized, there is still a risk that employers will discriminate against those whose qualifications are not awarded by an institution based within the EU.

Transparency and Recognition of Qualifications for Migrants

In view of the potential labor and skills shortages in some EU member states, a gradual policy change is taking place regarding the legal recruitment of migrants according to European labor-market needs. Detailed knowledge of the education and training systems of partner countries in terms of levels, content, and quality is therefore required, and policies and tools for transparency and recognition of qualifications are becoming an important issue (for both the EU and partner countries). The following is a brief overview of the existing tools for qualification recognition and some practical policy recommendations that can be taken into consideration by the EU in the implementation of mobility partnerships.

Recognition of Qualifications: Basic Definitions

Recognition of qualifications covers two main areas: academic and professional. The recognition of academic qualifications allows for the continuation of studies at the appropriate level. In the case of professional qualifications, recognition gives an individual the opportunity to practice his or her professional skills abroad. Professional and academic recognition is an administrative process in which the credentials of migrants are checked, but migrants themselves are not assessed.

Professional recognition covers both regulated and unregulated professions. Regulated professions[14] are governed by legal acts and imply automatic professional recognition. There is therefore automatic recognition among EU member states. The EU directive on the recognition of professional qualifications addresses the mutual recognition of professional qualifications.[15] The degree of regulation varies between member states. The following professions have been harmonized at the EU level: medical doctor, nurse, dentist, veterinary surgeon, midwife, pharmacist, and architect.

Most occupations and professions are not regulated. Unregulated professions do not legally require any specific process, because the employer can assess the qualifications and professional competency. But in many cases both individual migrants and employers will still seek advice on the value of the migrants' qualifications.

The recognition process is always a comparative process in which a migrant's qualifications are compared with qualifications in the host country. The migrant's qualifications are therefore not recognized on their own merits, but rather in relation to the national standards. A perfect match between the migrant's qualifications and the qualifications in the host country is unlikely, since qualifications have been developed in specific contexts, which do vary. The concept of "best fit" is used to decide whether qualifications are equivalent. The recognition process often results in partial recognition. In this case, additional evidence is required in order to prove that the migrant is fully qualified. Further study is often the consequence. This shows that professional recognition and academic recognition are linked processes.

The recognition of prior learning is a different process. Prior learning covers both nonformal and informal learning. Nonformal learning takes place outside educational institutions (schools, colleges, training centers, and universities), often at work, and does not lead to any certificates. Informal learning is part of everyday life and is not necessarily intentional. Recognition, accreditation, or validation of nonformal and informal learning is a process whereby an individual's learning achievements are compared with a national standard or qualification.

International Agreements and Processes for Qualification Recognition

Several international agreements, conventions, and processes have been launched, signed, or implemented in the field of transparency and recognition of qualifications, thus facilitating the mobility of students and workers. The following section is a brief overview of the most important initiatives in this field.

Bologna process. The Bologna Declaration was signed in June 1999 and was aimed at harmonizing degree structures and quality assurance procedures across higher-education systems, forming the European Higher Education Area (EHEA).[16] The Framework of Qualifications for the European Higher Education Area (FEHEA) is a metaframework for the national higher-education qualifications frameworks of the Bologna signatories. It contains descriptors for the three main cycles of higher-education qualifications, corresponding to BA, MA, and PhD degrees. Membership has grown beyond the geographical borders of the EU to include 46 nations.[17] In addition, the European Credit Transfer and Accumulation System (ECTS)[18] is a standard for comparing the study attainment and performance of students of higher education across the EU and other collaborating European countries.

Further geographical expansion is unlikely, since membership in the Bologna process is open only to countries that are party to the European Cultural Convention.[19] There are two ways in which the Bologna process is currently influencing higher-education reforms outside Europe: through tools such as the Diploma Supplement,[20] and, in other countries, the implementation of the three-cycle Bologna model.

Although further expansion of the EHEA is unlikely in the near future, cooperation beyond borders is now very much a part of the Bologna agenda. One example of the impact that the Bologna process is having beyond the borders of the EHEA is in the French-speaking countries of the Maghreb (Algeria, Morocco, and Tunisia). With higher education modeled on the French system, all three countries are adapting their higher-education systems to the Bologna-inspired French qualifications framework.

Copenhagen process. The Copenhagen Declaration was signed in 2002 to enhance cooperation in vocational education and training in Europe.[21] Under the Declaration, the member states, the European Economic Area countries, the social partners, and the European Commission have cooperated on several specific instruments, including agreements on common messages; references; and tools relating to transparency, quality assurance, validation, recognition of nonformal and informal learning, and vocational guidance; and on the development of a European Credit System for Vocational Education and Training (ECVET).[22] The geographical coverage of the Copenhagen process includes the future member states of the EU.[23]

European Qualifications Framework (EQF) for lifelong learning. The EQF is a common European reference framework that links countries' qualification systems, acting as a translation tool to make qualifications more transparent.[24] It has two principal aims: to promote mobility between countries and to facilitate lifelong learning. The EQF describes the expected results of learning as "learning outcomes," defined as what a person knows, understands, and is able to do, rather than time spent studying. The EQF has eight levels of complexity. The highest four levels coincide with the Bologna cycles, but can also include non-higher-education qualifications.

Europass. This is an EU initiative designed to increase the transparency of qualifications and the mobility of citizens in Europe.[25] It consists of five documents (CV, language passport, Europass mobility, certificate supplement, and diploma supplement) that should make a person's skills and qualifications clearly understood. The provision of good-quality information and guidance is an important factor in the improved transparency of qualifications and competences. The existing services and networks already play a valuable role that could be enhanced through closer cooperation to reinforce the added value of EU action.

UNESCO conventions. Under the aegis of UNESCO, five regional and one interregional convention for the recognition of higher-education studies and qualifications have been adopted.[26] Under the Council of Europe/UNESCO Convention (1997), national information centers were established as part of the European Network of Information Centres on academic mobility and recognition (ENIC[27]). To date, the attempts of UNESCO to transform the conventions into a universal instrument for qualification recognition have not been entirely successful.

WTO GATS mode 4. The General Agreement on Trade in Services (GATS) covers, among other issues, the temporary movement of service providers.[28] This implies gaining access to the labor markets in other countries, thus requiring the recognition of qualifications. The GATS encourages bilateral or plurilateral agreements on qualification recognition. The WTO Council on Trade in Services should be notified about any new recognition agreements, so that other member states can negotiate similar arrangements.

Challenges for Qualification Recognition within Legal Labor Migration Schemes

Qualification recognition remains an unresolved issue that is relevant for potential and returning migrants. According to ETF research on migration and skills, there appears to be no knowledge among migrants about the opportunities for professional and academic recognition and the recognition of prior learning. There also appear to be no processes in home countries to recognize skills obtained in EU countries during the migration experience. The migrants do not appear able to translate their experiences in the EU into improved human resources development opportunities on their return.

Fully understanding the challenges of qualification recognition for migrants requires that the issues facing the education and training systems of partner countries be highlighted. In order to respond to continually changing labor-market demands, education and training should be provided within a lifelong learning context: people of all ages should have equal and open access to quality learning opportunities, which is currently not always the case in most of the developing world.

One important issue is that continual education or adult training is either not sufficiently developed or completely absent. This situation is explained not only by the lack of a conceptual framework, but also by the fact that it has been given little or no attention by employers. It is often the case that training takes years, and by the time the workers have completed the course of study, labor demands have already changed. Furthermore, training is structured in a way that requires individuals to focus on already familiar or indeed irrelevant competencies and does not allow them to select what they really need. Training delivery that is competency-based and modular, which it is not at present, would offer individuals the opportunity to acquire only those competencies that are required at that moment, over relatively short periods of time.

Whether training is undertaken in a classroom, a workshop, the workplace, or a combination of these, it can result in qualifications that are recognizable, portable, and consistent at national level. One of the tools for assessing qualifications is the development of a qualifications framework that sets out the levels against which a qualification can be recognized. The accreditation of qualifications ensures that they are of a high quality and that they meet the needs of both learners and employers. Given this background, it is unrealistic to have a qualifications framework in the short to medium term that can be linked to the EQF. The creation of such a framework is a long-term process.

The tools described above refer mainly to the formal education system, but recognition of prior (nonformal or informal) learning is also viewed as a means of enhancing employability and career prospects. Validation of prior learning has not been developed in partner countries. There are initiatives in the OECD member states on the Recognition of Non-Formal and Informal Learning (RNFIL). In Denmark, regional knowledge centers for the documentation and recognition of prior learning for refugees and migrants have been opened, using e-tools (databases on job offers, on competence documentation and assessment, on a digital competence card, and so on). In the Netherlands, a center for international recognition and certification (for higher education) has been created, with assistance given in the preparation of a personal development plan. In Norway, a recognition system specifically for refugees has been put in place. The most comprehensive EU document in the field of RNFIL is Conclusions of the Council on Common European Principles for the Identification and Validation of Non-Formal and Informal Learning.[29] However, its contents are still too general and need more specification. The identification, anticipation, and monitoring of skills are challenges in partner countries. There is no single formula for skill needs analysis. However, experience from longstanding EU member states (EU15) has shown that what proved to be useful is a holistic approach, a combination of qualitative analysis (such as case studies and focus group discussions) and quantitative data (including surveys, skill audits, and econometric models). This approach can be applied at all levels: regional, sectoral, and occupational. In partner countries, conventional skills forecasting methods are either nonexistent or not considered sufficiently reliable, often because of poor-quality data that are, in the main, out of date. Furthermore, the speed of economic transformation and the existence of a large informal sector are factors that make the process of skills identification even more difficult. Experience demonstrates that skill needs analyses in partner countries are often limited to ad hoc donor initiatives that remain at the level of pilots and are not implemented regularly.

Capitalizing on the Skills of Returning Migrants

The return of migrants, even return that is temporary or virtual, can play a useful role in fostering the transfer of skills to the developing world, as well as other forms of brain circulation. The ETF migration survey confirms a general trend in which there is a mismatch between the level of education or skills held by migrants and the job performed in host countries. This is significantly less prominent in the context of the bilateral arrangements that exist among Egypt and Tunisia and the Gulf States. There is also an agreement with Italy that involves an annual quota system and is based on skills. These examples are rare, and there are issues linked to their implementation. There are ongoing negotiations on managed labor migration schemes. However, the process has been slow, and the host countries have faced political resistance at home from those who fear competition from cheap foreign labor. Aside from such instances, it is common to observe, for example, in the case of Moldovan workers, that the jobs performed abroad by migrants did not correspond to the level of education and skills they possessed (if recognized). This is mainly because of the following factors:

- *Labor demand in the host countries.* This could be managed through bilateral labor agreements between the home and host countries, by identifying the skill needs of the host labor markets, and by adequately preparing migrants to respond to these requirements. Here, predeparture training can play an important role. The implementation of the Canadian federal and provincial skill works programs is an example of regulated migration. Another is the positive and proactive attitude developed by the Tunisian Agency for Technical Cooperation in assisting the regulated migration of medium- and highly skilled Tunisians to the labor-importing countries of the Gulf.

- **Illegality.** Illegal migrants have a weaker position in host labor markets and are often forced to accept low-qualified and low-paid jobs. Increasing legal opportunities should be coupled with information campaigns on the risks of illegal migration. The IDOM[30] project, promoted by Egyptian and Italian authorities in cooperation with the Egyptian media, is an example of good practice to be followed by others.

The number of the returning migrants who become employers or self-employed is significant.[31] The best way to encourage return migration is a combination of government policies and a vibrant economy at home. In order to promote the role of returning migrants in local development, policy makers need to carefully target return schemes that can facilitate job creation. Currently these schemes are rarely available and hardly used.

Options and Tools: Short- Versus Medium- and Long-Term
Given the complex background of the education and training systems in partner countries, assessing qualifications from these parts of the world is a real challenge. In the short and medium terms, it will not be possible to take the necessary profound steps toward reforms in these education and training systems.

Points for Action

Actions can be proposed in the short, medium, and long term for two specific target groups: potential migrants and returning migrants.

Potential Migrants
In the short term, actions can just focus on information activities through specific centers or campaigns. Nevertheless, pilot actions could be implemented as well, in order to prepare the field for more ambitious policies.

Short-term actions. Information centers should be established to evaluate qualifications and provide advice and information on recognition matters. The centers would not certify credentials or qualifications, but would provide services that draw on information and knowledge that is available within a sector or region and from other countries. The aim would be to disseminate information and guidance on the recognition of skills and qualifications in specific countries. The advice would relate to academic and professional qualifications, as well as to the ways in which informal learning could be documented in order for it to be recognized within national qualification structures. One solution would be to host the center within the network of the national employment services. Creating new institutions is costly, but capacity building could be provided to the existing ones.

- Referral centers (or contact centers) could be established to help expatriates in specific professions make contact with migrants. The expatriates could share information and experiences that might be useful in obtaining recognition of qualifications, and provide details of the extent to which experience and skills match particular jobs or educational programs. Again, inclusion of these facilities within the national employment services network would strengthen the system.

- Information campaigns on the risks of illegal migration need to be promoted, and should address the risk of exploitation and skill waste.

- On the bilateral level, pilot actions may improve qualification in priority sectors for migration (such as construction and agriculture) or regulated professions (for example, nursing). However, care should be taken that such initiatives do not remain isolated, but are incorporated in a systemic approach to qualification recognition.

Medium- and long-term actions

- At the national level it will be important to provide capacity building for skill needs analysis; this should be part of the overall improvement of labor-market information systems. This will help partner countries to move to more evidence-based employment and human resources policies. The main institutions to be targeted should be the labor ministries and the national employment services.

- Efforts to improve skills identification and matching should be combined with broader education, training, and labor-market reforms aimed at strengthening governance. It is important for the EU to promote coordination among ministries in policy development, in particular the labor, education, and economy ministries, and to help them to reflect together on where they want their economy to be, to decide on the sectors they would like to develop, and to build a manpower policy accordingly. These harmonized efforts will also foster more precise information flows between the education system and the labor market, which in turn will facilitate skills analysis. Furthermore, the EU should provide support to tripartite advisory bodies and to individual social partners in policy planning, development, and implementation in order to help them to fulfill their role. All these efforts will require parallel investments in education and labor-market reforms.

- It is important to identify and agree upon standards for sector skills with social partners. These standards should reflect the local realities but also the international situation. This will facilitate qualification recognition in the future, but it also is part of the effort for the establishment of a qualifications framework. Some partner countries have established, with varying degrees of success, national skills standards in some sectors. The issue is that this type of work is usually donor driven and is not extended to the entire education system. In addition, the education and training systems are not automatically able to transform the skills standards into education standards. Hence, there is a temptation for some donors to concentrate their efforts in specific schools, which then are used as a pool for potential migrants.

- Opportunities to learn from European experience could be of great interest to partner countries. For example, awareness-raising seminars and workshops such as the European Qualifications Framework (EQF) could be organized.

- The national authorities of home countries need to be supported and encouraged to gain inspiration from the Copenhagen and Bologna processes. Moreover, EU member states should start thinking about how these processes can be extended to interested partner countries. As a first step, these countries could be invited as observers.

- Work on the preparation of national skills standards should take place in tripartite sector committees. These committees should be involved in similar processes with the relevant counterparts from interested member states in order to identify the comparability of standards between countries. In order to make this an operational solution, the best way to proceed would be within the framework of bilateral agreements.

- Predeparture training should not only cover language and cultural orientation, but should also be extended to include the upgrading of professional skills in line with agreed skills standards.

Returning Migrants

In the short term, information is crucial to facilitate returning migrants' reintegration. In particular, they should be aware of their potential business opportunities. In the medium to long term, qualification recognition could help them for a better use of the skills acquired abroad.

Short-term actions. Reaping the benefits of return migration does not happen automatically. Countries need to offer effective reintegration programs for potential returning migrants, including better reception and advice on investment opportunities and access to business support and credits for entrepreneurship.

Medium- and long-term actions

- In order to exploit fully the potential of returning migrants for local development, policy makers in home countries should establish a system for the recognition of qualifications and the validation of nonformal and informal learning. As the ETF migration survey demonstrates, on-the-job training was the most common type of training abroad, and a system of recognition should be put in place to capitalize fully on this. The improvement of education and training systems in sending countries should be one of the priority areas of investment for future EU intervention.

- A preliminary condition to exploit this potential is to develop an efficient business environment. This includes instituting measures to limit administrative burden for business, to create an efficient finance system, and to reduce the costs of doing business, but also creating attitudes for business through entrepreneurship education.

Notes

1. http://www.ilo.org/public/english/protection/migrant/papers/migmagh/ch1.htm.
2. For example, Egypt allows dual nationality if the other country concerned permits it. The Egyptian Law on Nationality of 1975 was modified in 2004 to allow Egyptian women married to foreigners (regardless of their nationality) to pass on their citizenship to their children. Tunisians are also allowed to have dual nationality, in particular with France. Legislation has also been developed to avoid a situation in which people with dual citizenship would be obliged

to undertake military or social service in both countries (for example, the convention signed March 18, 1982, modified July 12, 2007, between France and Tunisia). Since 2002, Moldova has allowed dual nationality, but individuals included in this group cannot become members of Parliament (Law No. 273 of April 10, 2008). Dual citizenship is also allowed for Albanians, according to Article 3 of the Law on Citizenship of 1991, but men are obliged to undertake Albanian military service.

3. Tunisia has bilateral social security agreements with France, Belgium, Algeria, the Netherlands, Libya, Austria, Italy, Germany, and Luxembourg (http://www.tunisia.com/tunisia/business/employment-issues). In addition, it has a similar agreement as part of the European—Mediterranean Partnership (EMP).

4. Available at http://www.etf.europa.eu.

5. The quota was set at 7,000 workers in 2006 and at 8,000 in 2007. Information from Italian Interior Ministry, 2007, available at http://www.interno.it/mininterno/export/sites/default/it/assets/files/15/0673_Rapporto_immigrazione_BARBAGLI.pdf.

6. Integrated Migration Information Service (http://www.emigration.gov.eg). This project has involved the development and maintenance of an online database of Egyptians working abroad and a Web site (Misirat) providing information on legal migration opportunities in European countries.

7. Information Dissemination on Migration.

8. http://europa.eu/rapid/pressReleasesAction.do?reference=IP/08/893&.

9. Information from the Italian Interior Ministry (2007). http://www.interno.it/mininterno/export/sites/default/it/assets/files/15/0673_Rapporto_immigrazione_BARBAGLI.pdf.

10. UNESCO Institute of Statistics database: http://www.uis.unesco.org.

11. Bahrain, Kuwait, Oman, Qatar, Saudi Arabia, and the United Arab Emirates.

12. This caveat is important, since it appears quite plausible that more skilled migrants to the EU may have been able to integrate better into the EU labor market, and so may have been less likely to return.

13. See, for example, S. M. Aminuzamman, "Migration of skilled nurses from Bangladesh," DRC Research Report, Development Research Centre on Migration, Globalisation and Poverty, University of Sussex, Brighton, 2007.

14. EC directive on the recognition of professional qualifications: 2005/36/EC.

15. For an overview of the procedure, see http://www.nuffic.nl/nederlandse-organisaties/services/docs/beroepserkenning/flowchart-nieuwe-richtlijn.pdf.

16. http://ec.europa.eu/education/policies/educ/bologna/bologna_en.html.

17. Member states of the Bologna process: Albania, Andorra, Armenia, Austria, Azerbaijan, Belgium, Bosnia and Herzegovina, Bulgaria, Croatia, Cyprus, Czech

Republic, Denmark, Estonia, Finland, France, Georgia, Germany, Greece, Holy See, Hungary, Iceland, Ireland, Italy, Latvia, Liechtenstein, Lithuania, Luxembourg, Malta, Moldova, Montenegro, the Netherlands, Norway, Poland, Portugal, Romania, Russian Federation, Serbia, Slovak Republic, Slovenia, Spain, Sweden, Switzerland, the former Yugoslav Republic of Macedonia, Turkey, Ukraine, United Kingdom.

18. http://ec.europa.eu./education/programmes/socrates/ects/index_en.html.

19. http://conventions.coe.int/Treaty/EN/Treaties/Html/018.htm.

20. http://ec.europa.eu/education/policies/rec_qual/recognition/diploma_en .html.

21. http://ec.europa.eu/education/policies/2010/vocational_en.html.

22. http://ec.europa.eu/education/policies/2010/doc/ecvt2005_en.pdf. ECVET is a system of accumulation and transfer of credits, designed for vocational education and training in Europe.

23. Croatia, the former Yugoslav Republic of Macedonia, and Turkey.

24. http://ec.europa.eu/education/policies/educ/eqf/index_en.html The EQF is a tool designed to compare the levels of qualifications (course certificates, professional certificates, and so forth) among different European countries. The EQF is divided into eight reference levels, where level one corresponds to the completion of compulsory school and level eight to a PhD.

25. http://europass.cedefop.europa.eu/europass/preview.action?locale_id=1.

26. http://portal.unesco.org/education/en/ev.php-URL_ID=22124&URL_DO= DO_TOPIC&URL_SECTION=201.html.

27. http://www.enic-naric.net.

28. http://www.wto.org/english/tratop_e/serv_e/gatsintr_e.htm.

29. http://ec.europa.eu/education/policies/2010/doc/validation2004_en.pdf.

30. http://www.utlcairo.org/stampa/imm_en.pdf.

31. According to the ETF migration survey, except in Moldova, most returning migrants became employers or self-employed: 50 percent in Albania, 41 percent in Egypt, and 57 percent in Tunisia.

CHAPTER 4

Conclusions and Recommendations

This report aims to unravel the complex relationship between migration and skills development, an area that has not always received the attention it deserves. It paints a precise picture of potential and returning migrants from four very different countries—Albania, Egypt, Moldova, and Tunisia—and describes the skills they possess and the impact that the experience of migration has on their skills development. By doing so, it aims to promote a better understanding of the phenomenon of migration and the human faces behind it—who they are and what they can offer, both to the countries they migrate to and to their countries of origin when they return. It also offers suggestions on how the governments of countries sending migrants and of those receiving migrants, particularly in the EU, could move toward more effective policies for managing migration flows for the benefit of all.

One of the main conclusions of this report is that there is a significant mismatch between the skills migrants possess and the jobs they end up doing while abroad, especially in the case of people who migrate to the EU. This waste of human potential, or brain waste, is a particular problem for Albanians and Moldovans, because more than 60 percent of these migrants worked abroad as unskilled workers regardless of their qualifications.

The phenomenon of brain waste is the result of many factors. These include the nature of demand for labor in receiving countries, the lack or inefficient implementation of bilateral agreements to manage the flow of migrants, problems related to quality of education in sending countries, and whether the qualifications they produce are recognized by receiving countries. The extent of illegal migration is another powerful factor, as illegal migrants are usually in a weaker position than people who are there legally and often have to accept worse jobs and conditions as a result. Finally, the report highlights the difference that informal networks abroad can make to migrants. Well-established communities abroad, such as the Tunisian community in France, can help new arrivals to find better jobs. Expatriate communities from countries such as Moldova or Albania, who have only recently experienced mass migration, have less to offer to their compatriots.

While all four sending countries surveyed in this report have reasonably comprehensive policies in place to support migration, the way they are implemented limits their effectiveness. This means that migrants still mainly follow market incentives and use informal channels to organize their migration experience. There is a need for better organization of, and publicity for, migration schemes, including making good use of informal networks such as existing migrant communities. Organized schemes for outward migration that could match skills levels to demand are particularly lacking.

The issue of brain waste is especially acute in the case of migration to the EU. The ETF survey confirmed earlier findings such as that of Fargues (2005) that highly skilled migrants tend to prefer to migrate to North America, or, in the case of Egyptians, to the Gulf rather than to the EU. Greece and Italy stand out as destinations especially likely to attract low-skilled migrants. Only in the case of Moldovans is the pattern different. Here, individuals with lower skills levels were more likely to be planning to go to Russia than to the EU. However, even with Moldovans, there was a significant amount of low-skilled migration to Europe. It is important to note that those who were planning to go to the EU had low expectations of being able to use their skills at an appropriate level. A look at the jobs done by returning migrants confirms this expectation; over 55 percent of migrants to the EU found only unskilled work and only 7.2 percent worked as managers or professionals.

This finding suggests that the EU is losing the global competition to attract the best-qualified, most capable migrants, something that could have significant consequences for the EU's competitiveness in the long term. The report mentions some bilateral initiatives that are trying to lessen the skills mismatch by providing job-specific training for migrants, such as a scheme to train Albanian nurses to work in northern Italy. However, this scheme also illustrates some of the difficulties of such initiatives. Gaining Italian recognition for Albanian nursing diplomas entails high transaction costs for the migrants involved, which may not be affordable. Even after someone's qualification has been officially recognized, the risk of discrimination by employers unconvinced by foreign diplomas remains.

All this indicates that more concerted action to promote easier recognition of the qualifications of migrants is required. Because of potential skills shortages in some EU countries, the EU as a whole is becoming more receptive to the idea of legal recruitment of migrants to fill these gaps. Developing tools that can give transparency and facilitate the recognition of the qualifications of migrants is becoming an important issue for both EU and partner countries. Although designed for internal use, processes such as Bologna and Copenhagen and tools such as the European Qualifications Framework are having an impact beyond the borders of the EU and could prove useful in the context of migration. Other initiatives such the European Commission's proposal for a blue-card scheme to attract highly skilled migrants are also welcome.

The report suggests various initiatives that sending and receiving countries may consider in the short term in order to provide a better deal for potential migrants. Governments in sending countries could set up dedicated information centers to assess migrants' qualifications and provide advice on recognition in different destinations. This advice should cover not only formal academic and professional qualifications but also inform people how to document and demonstrate nonformal learning. The centers could be housed within the existing network of national employment offices to lessen the costs of such a venture. Referral centers could also be set up to put would-be migrants in touch with expatriates working in a specific trade or profession who can provide up-to-date information and advice. There should be information campaigns warning people of the dangers involved in illegal migration, and this should also cover the risk of exploitation and skill waste. Finally, pilot actions to enable bilateral recognition of qualifications in priority areas such as construction, agriculture, and regulated professions such as nursing should be undertaken. Care must be taken that these actions do not remain isolated examples, but instead act as forerunners for a systemic approach to recognizing qualifications.

Measures for the medium and longer term could include a drive to improve the capacity for skills needs analysis in sending countries as part of an overall move to improve information systems on the labor market. Efforts to improve skills identification and matching should be combined with broader moves aimed at strengthening governance of the education and training system and finding more effective ways of intervening in the labor market. The EU should help promote better coordination among the ministries of education, labor, and economy when developing policy and when setting national priorities for economic development. If a more coordinated approach is achieved, this would also lead to a better flow of information between the education system and the labor market, and facilitate the task of skills needs analysis.

Social partners in sending countries should be encouraged to participate in defining skills standards for different sectors of the economy as part of a tripartite process. These should pay attention to both local and international needs. Such moves, already under way in some sectors in some of the ETF's partner countries, could facilitate the recognition of qualifications in the future and lay the foundations for national qualifications frameworks. For example, stakeholders in partner countries should be encouraged to learn from European experience in qualifications recognition by being invited to attend events on the European Qualifications Framework.

This report shows that returning migrants do have the potential to make a positive contribution to development in their countries of origin. But as things stand, they do not receive the support they need when they return, and thus their impact on local development is still limited. In general, it seems that the best way to encourage migrants to return home is a combination of a vibrant economy, a good climate for business, and sensible government policy tailored to their needs. This includes better reception arrangements, advice on investment opportunities, and support for entrepreneurship. The issue of recognition of skills and qualifications is also important. Currently, there are no mechanisms in countries of origin for recognizing the skills that migrants may have acquired while they were abroad, with the exception of higher education in some cases. How to validate skills acquired outside the formal education system is a particular concern, because most migrants gain their skills on the job. Governments should do more to maintain contact with their nationals while they are abroad; the efforts of the Tunisian government in this respect provide one positive example of how this could be done.

The relationship between migration and skills development is a complex one. As this report shows, improving the situation would involve short- and longer-term action involving a wide range of actors in both sending and receiving countries. In particular, improving the conditions in which migrants leave their countries of origin, work abroad, and return home contributes to a win-win situation for everyone.

Methodology and Data Representativity Assessment

Sampling Design

A two-stage cluster sample was selected. First-stage clusters were a minimum of four to six regions chosen to represent the geographical diversity of the country, and second-stage clusters were villages, communes, or municipalities chosen to represent the geographical diversity of the selected regions. The detail of each cluster selection was agreed upon with each local service provider, such that at both stages (selection of regions, and selection of villages, communes, or municipalities), areas with high and low levels of development, areas of high and low levels of international migration, and both rural and urban areas were included.

The procedure for selecting individual interviewees varied for potential migrants and returning migrants. Potential migrants' households were selected by interviewers following random routes. Within each household, interviewers chose the interviewee through random procedures (that is, by taking the person whose month of birth fell next after completion of the interview), in order to minimize any selection bias.

Nevertheless, circumstances in Egypt led to the decision to ignore the intent to establish national representation in some cases. This resulted in some villages and governorates being oversampled in order to increase coverage of potential migrants to Europe. In addition, individuals outside the labor force who were not studying full time were excluded. The latter added to the anticipation that males would be overrepresented in Egypt.

In order to identify and select returning migrants, local companies followed the "snow-ball" technique. Even if more than one household member met the criteria to be surveyed, only one was interviewed. He or she was selected randomly (for example, according to the "closest birthday" procedure).

This sampling methodology produced the following expectations:

- The potential migration survey should be broadly representative of the young adult population (ages 18–40) as a whole. Thus, in principle, roughly equal numbers of men and women had to be interviewed.
- The return migration survey might have some bias toward men (because it is generally accepted that more men would have migrated).

Fieldwork was carried out during November and December 2006. The survey on potential migrants resulted in a total sample size of 3,834 respondents—998 from Albania, 812 from Egypt, 1,009 from Moldova, and 1,015 from Tunisia. A total of 4,010 returning migrants were interviewed: 1,000 each in Albania, Egypt, and Tunisia, and 1,010 in Moldova.

Margin of Error and Difficulties Encountered During the Fieldwork

Assuming a simple random sampling, for a confidence level of 95 percent and p=q=0.5, table A1.1 shows the margin of error for different numbers of answers,[1] for one country.

The so-called gender gap was the most common problem encountered by interviewers. In Egypt, Tunisia, and to a lesser extent Albania, fewer women than men were interviewed. This had been expected for the returning migrants' survey (see above), but not particularly for potential migrants. This is the result of cultural factors and the nature of the migration phenomenon in these national contexts. There is a widespread belief that

Table A1.1   Margin of Error per Number of Answers

Number of answers	1,000	750	500	250	125	100	50
Margin of error	3.1%	3.6%	4.4%	6.2%	8.8%	9.8%	13.9%

Source: ETF survey data.

migration concerns primarily the (male) head of household, or men in general. For that reason, men were more often the respondents to the survey.

The returning migration survey encountered additional problems. In Albania the number of returning migrants who fulfilled the conditions was limited. Consequently, it was difficult to select sufficient numbers randomly within families. Hence, a large proportion of the returning migrants were surveyed in public places or workplaces. Most of the respondents of this category were men. As a result, the survey of returning migrants has a noticeable disparity between the numbers of men and women.

In Moldova, the company in charge of the fieldwork explained that for the returning-migrants survey there was a high number of refusals for two main reasons: fear of being robbed (as they had returned with money), and fear of being approached by law enforcement agencies (when they had worked illegally).

Data Representation and Other Data Issues

Given the issues that arose during the interview process, the data were analyzed with regard to representativity, and the respective national populations in the survey were compared to other data sources from the country (census and surveys) and UN population data. For Egypt, comparison with other data shows that men are highly overrepresented, a problem mentioned above. In addition, young people are greatly overrepresented for both men and women. In the case of Tunisia, men in general are highly overrepresented, compared to the Tunisian population as a whole. Furthermore, based on UN data, men are overrepresented in their mid-20s and women in their early 20s, while census data show comparable ages for men, with only women tending to be younger. It was not possible to assess education (because of a lack of comparable data). However, it can be said that the illiteracy rate in the census is much higher than in the sample, indicating that the people in the sample are generally better educated.

The sample of Albanians also differs from the country's population as a whole, though not to such an extent. The analysis shows that men are overrepresented in the sample. The comparison of the age distribution illustrates that individuals in the sample tend to be younger than the national population. This is caused by a high overrepresentation of young men in the sample; the women in the sample are slightly older on average than those in the national population. With respect to education, people of both sexes with primary education, but especially women, are underrepresented, suggesting that the individuals in the survey are better educated than the Albanian population of the corresponding age group.

Representativity in the sample from Moldova is much better in terms of age and gender, and more questionable when it comes to education. Educated people are overrepresented and individuals with general secondary education are underrepresented. An analysis by gender reveals that men with vocational education are highly oversampled; females are highly underrepresented in primary education and overrepresented in vocational and university education.

More generally it should be noted that most data dealing with migration are subject to potential bias. This is because migrants, and consequently also potential migrants, may be selected by certain unobservable characteristics compared to nonmigrants. The analysis will control for as many characteristics as the set of variables allows, though obviously it is not possible to cover those that are unobservable. For a more extensive discussion of selection bias in migration data, see, for example, Constant and Massey (2003), Borjas (1991), or Chiquiar and Hanson (2005).

Overall, the survey design and the resulting data have produced a very rich set of variables, and the data provide interesting information in an area for which data have not been available up until now. Nevertheless, representativity in relation to the national population remains a critical problem when it comes to migrant profiles, and it is necessary to keep in mind the sources of potential bias when examining the results and in the subsequent analysis. It should also be emphasized that this analysis is based on data from four particular countries and results may not necessarily apply to migrants from other countries.

Note

1. The results of a survey include a statistical margin of error caused by the sampling process. This margin varies according to three factors:
    - the sample size—the greater the number of respondents to a question, the smaller the margin of error.
    - the result itself—the closer the result is to 50 percent, the wider the statistical margin will be. This is expressed by 'p=q=0.5'. It represents the higher margin of error, or its upper limit for the answer to a question.
    - the degree of confidence—in the social sciences, the most widely used degree of confidence is 95 percent.

Statistical Tables

All tables are based on the results of the ETF survey. Data from the econometric analysis are available from the ETF upon request. Also see Avato (2009).

Table A2.1   Preparedness for Migration among Potential Migrants

	Albania (% / N)	Egypt, Arab Rep. (% / N)	Moldova (% / N)	Tunisia (% / N)
Have a passport	71.7/428	44.4/362	78.9/446	75.7/636
Have sufficient information about most likely destination country	62.0/442	75.5/384	55.2/446	60.6/632
Able to finance move abroad	58.4/442	62.0/384	40.6/446	53.5/637
Speak official language of most likely destination country fluently or fairly well	29.2/442	52.9/384	45.6/441	56.3/628
Have health certificate	14.7/428	17.2/47	14.3/446	12.4/610
Have proof of study or training already completed	2.6/428	61.3/111	4.0/446	6.4/607
Have visa	7.5/428	4.4/268	5.4/446	1.3/617
Have work contract	4.9/428	3.7/160	5.6/446	1.8/610
No problems expected in getting necessary documents	25.2/413	54.5/365	28.4/433	13.5/626

Table A2.2 Potential Migrants' Level of Education and Expectations of the Level of Employment That They Might Obtain Abroad

Country	Level of education	Other	Professional	High management	Middle management	Skilled worker	Unskilled worker	Don't know	N
					Work level (%)				
Albania	Low		1.9			21.5	65.2	11.4	158
	Medium		6.8		0.5	36.7	49.3	6.8	221
	High		31.6		1.8	50.9	12.3	3.5	57
	Total		8.3		0.5	33.0	50.2	8.0	436
Egypt, Arab Rep.	Low			2.2	4.4	64.4	28.9		45
	Medium	0.5	21.3	4.3	8.2	42.5	23.2		207
	High		57.6	9.1	20.5	7.6	5.3		132
	Total	0.3	31.3	5.7	12.0	33.1	17.7		384
Moldova	Low		3.4		0.7	18.7	61.9	18.7	134
	Medium				1.7	33.9	44.6	16.3	233
	High		10.5	1.8	3.5	28.1	43.9	12.3	57
	Total		3.3	0.2	1.7	28.3	50.0	16.5	424
Tunisia	Low	0.7	4.3		3.6	51.1	27.3	12.9	139
	Medium	0.4	7.1	9.2	11.8	45.8	17.6	8.0	238
	High	1.4	11.4	24.8	25.7	14.8	7.1	14.8	210
	Total	0.9	8.0	12.6	14.8	35.9	16.2	11.6	587

Table A2.3 Returning Migrants: Longest Job Abroad by Educational Level

Country	Level of education	Other	Professional	Senior management	Middle management	Skilled worker	Unskilled worker	Don't know	No answer	N
Albania	Low	0.6	0.3	0.0	0.0	18.1	80.3		0.6	315
	Medium	0.4	2.0	0.7	1.1	27.8	67.6		0.5	561
	High	1.6	13.7	0.0	1.6	18.5	63.7		0.8	124
	Total	0.6	2.9	0.4	0.8	23.6	71.1		0.6	1,000
Egypt, Arab Rep.	Low		0.0	1.0	3.8	73.2	22.0			209
	Medium		6.8	2.9	14.4	56.2	19.6			409
	High		64.1	13.6	10.5	7.3	4.5			382
	Total		27.3	6.6	10.7	41.1	14.3			1,000
Moldova	Low	1.2	1.2		0	22.8	73.2	1.6	1.2	250
	Medium		1.7		0.2	33.6	61.6	1.3	1.6	631
	High		3.9		1.6	23.3	69.0	0.0	2.3	129
	Total		1.9		0.3	29.6	65.4	1.2	1.6	1010
Tunisia	Low	1.1	5.9	0.9	3.7	56.9	30.4	0.4	0.7	543
	Medium	1.1	5.6	1.1	5.3	50.8	36.1	0.0	0.0	266
	High	1.9	11.5	15.4	32.7	25.0	12.5	1.0	0.0	104
	Total	1.2	6.5	2.6	7.4	51.5	30.0	0.3	0.4	913

Longest work level abroad (%)

Questionnaires of the Potential Migration and Return Migration Surveys

Potential Migration Survey

Serial No. ....
Interviewee Name: ....
Gender: 1. Male   (   )   2. Female   (   )
Governorate / District: .... City / Village: ....

Relationship to Head of Household

      1. Head of household   (   )   2. Spouse of HHH   (   )
      3. Son/Daughter of HHH   (   )   4. Grandson/daughter of HHH   (   )
      0. Other   (   )

Interview Date: / / 2006

Researcher Name: ....

Field Supervisor Name: ....

**All information provided is confidential and will be used only
for research purposes**

Introduction

This research is being conducted by ETF, an agency of the European Union. The purpose
is to understand the link between migration and the labour market education and training.
The results will be used for information for the development of migration and education

(continued)

policies. We would like to talk to you to find out your experience and opinions related to travelling abroad for work. Whatever we hear from you will only be used for the purposes of this research.

Now we would like to know if there is someone in the family who had returned from work abroad from 3 months or less than 10 years, for a period that exceeded 6 months of working abroad? Is there anybody with these specifications?

1. Yes
2. No

(1) In case there is no family member who had returned from work abroad from 3 months or less than 10 years for a period that exceeded 6 months of working abroad, ask about another family in the area that has a member that worked outside Egypt for a 6 months period or more and returned back from less than 10 years or more than 3 months.

- Name: ....
- Detailed Address: ....
  ....

(2) No. of household members: ....members

- No. of household members of aged 18 – 40 years (Egypt only: working or studying)

- How to choose: (1) nearest birth month (   )   (2) by chance (   )

Section A. Social and demographic characteristics and education

101.   How old are you? ____ ____ years

102.   What is your current marital status?
      1. Never married   ( )
      2. Engaged   ( )
      3. Married   ( )
      4. Widowed   ( )
      5. Divorced   ( )

103.   Do you have any children?
      1. Yes
      2. No → **Q105**

104.   How many? ____ child(ren)

105.   What is the highest level of education you have completed?
      1. Did not attend school   ( ) → **Q108**
      2. Less than Primary   ( ) → **Q108**
      3. Primary   ( ) → **Q108**
      4. Preparatory/Post-primary   ( ) → **Q108**   See explanatory notes
      5. Secondary General   ( )
      6. Secondary Vocational   ( )
      7. Post-secondary   ( )
      8. University   ( )

106. What was your field of study?
[to be coded according to ISCED fields after completion of interview]
....

107. Why did you choose this field of study? [Choose one reason only]
1. Personal interest   ( )
2. Encouraged by others   ( ) .
3. To get a job   ( )
4. To be able to go abroad   ( )
5. Because of the grades I obtained ( )
0. Other (specify)   ( )

108. Do you intend to do any further education or training?
1. Yes   ( )
2. No   ( ) → **Q 110**

109. If yes, in what field of study?
....

110. Do you think that education helps people to improve their living standards?
1. Yes   ( )
2. No   ( )
8. Don't know   ( )

111. Do you think it is important to invest in education?
1. Yes   ( )
2. No   ( )
8. Don't know   ( )

112. What language did you speak at home as a child?
....

113. Besides this language, which other languages do you speak?
1. None
2. English
3. French
4. Russian
5. Italian
6. Greek
7. Arabic
8. Romanian or Moldovan
0. Other (specify) ....

Section B. Work

We would now like to ask you some questions about your work.

201. Have you spent at least one hour in the last seven days in earning a living (working for pay)?
1. Yes   ( ) → **Q 205**
2. No   ( )

(continued)

202. Why are you not working?
     1. Holiday → **Q 205**
     2. Strike → **Q 205**
     3. Sick → **Q 205**
     4. Compulsory military service → **Q 205**
     5. Studying
     6. Cannot find work
     7. Do not need/want to work
     0. Other (specify) ....

203. Are you looking for work?
     1. Yes   (   )
     2. No   (   )

204. Have you ever worked?
     1. Yes   (   )
     2. No   (   ) → **Q301**

205. What work do (did) you do?
     [Prompt if more than one job/activity to describe main job/activity only here]
     [Insert three lists from explanatory notes if this will help interviewer]
     ....
     ....
     ....
     ....
     ....
     ....

206. Do you have other jobs beside this one?
     1. Yes   (   )
     2. No   (   )

207. In relation to all the work you do to earn money, how many hours do you normally
     work per week? .... hours

208. About how much money do you make per month (after tax), from all the work you do?
     .... Pounds/Dinars/Lek/Lei

Section C. Intentions

I'd now like to ask you some questions about your future intentions.

301. Are you thinking seriously to move abroad to live and work at the moment?
     1. Yes   (   ) → **Q401**
     2. No   (   )

302. Why are you not looking to move abroad?
     [Select up to **three** reasons **in the order they are mentioned**]
     1. This is my country/I belong here   (   )
     2. My family/relatives are here   (   )
     3. People are not friendly abroad   (   )

4. Discrimination in other countries   (   )
5. I would feel lonely abroad   (   )
6. Homesickness   (   )
7. Low incomes abroad   (   )
8. Poor work conditions abroad   (   )
9. Impossible or very difficult
   to find work abroad   (   )
0. Other/don't know (specify) .... **→ Q304**

303. What is the most important reason?
   ....
   ....

304. Do you think that people who have lived and worked abroad have experiences abroad that help them find better work opportunities when they return?
   1. Yes   (   )
   2. No   (   )
   8. Don't know   (   )

305. Do you think that returnees are better or worse off than those who didn't go abroad?
   1. Much better off   (   )
   2. Better off   (   )
   3. About the same   (   )
   4. Worse off   (   )
   5. Much worse off   (   )   See explanatory notes

306. Are you aware of any official programmes or schemes that allow people to work abroad?
   1. Yes (specify) ....   (   )
   2. No   (   )

Move to Q 501

Section D. Expectations

401. How likely or unlikely is it that you would leave (name survey country) within the next <u>6 months</u>?
   1. Very unlikely   (   )   See explanatory notes
   2. Quite unlikely   (   )
   3. Neither likely nor unlikely   (   )
   4. Quite likely   (   )
   5. Very likely   (   ) **→ also tick 'very likely' to Q402**

402. How likely or unlikely is it that you would leave (name survey country) within the next <u>2 years</u>?
   1. Very unlikely   (   )   See explanatory notes
   2. Quite unlikely   (   )
   3. Neither likely nor unlikely   (   )
   4. Quite likely   (   )
   5. Very likely   (   )

(continued)

403. If you were to leave (name survey country), please give me the reason(s) you would
have for leaving?
[insert list from explanatory notes if this will help interviewer]
[List up to **three** reasons **in the order they are mentioned**]
....
....

404. What is your most important reason?
....
....

405. Do you think the decision to move abroad would be made by you, or by others?
1. Entirely by you → **Q 407**   (   )
2. Made entirely by others   (   )
3. Both   (   )
8. Don't know → **Q 407**   (   )

406. Who else might influence your decision?
1. Parents   (   )
2. Spouse   (   )
3. Brothers/sisters   (   )
4. In-laws   (   )
5. Employer   (   )
6. Friend   (   )
0. Other (specify) ....

407. Do you think that moving abroad could improve your financial situation?
1. Yes   (   )
2. No   (   )
8. Don't know   (   )

408. If you were to move abroad, which country would you be most likely to go to?
...........................[= MLD]

409. How likely or unlikely is it that you would move to (name MLD) to live and work?
1. Very unlikely   (   )
2. Quite unlikely   (   )
3. Neither likely nor unlikely   (   )
3. Quite likely   (   )
4. Very likely   (   )   See explanatory notes

410. Why would you move to (name MLD)?
[insert list from explanatory notes if this will help interviewer]
[List up to **three** reasons **in the order they are mentioned**]
....
....

411. What is the most important reason?
....
....

412. Are you able to finance your move abroad?
    1. Yes   (   )
    2. No   (   )
    8. Don't know   (   )

413. Are you aware of any government programmes or companies that help people to work abroad?
    1. Government programmes   (   )
    2. Private recruitment companies   (   )
    3. Both of the above   (   )
    4. No → **Q416**   (   )

414. Do you think you will participate in these programmes or use these companies?
    1. Yes, only government scheme   (   ) → **Q416**
    2. Yes, only private company   (   ) → **Q416**
    3. Yes, both   (   ) → **Q416**
    4. No   (   )

415. Why would you not benefit?
    1. Not for the right kind of work   (   )
    2. I do not have the required
       qualifications   (   )
    3. No schemes for the country
       I want to go to   (   )
    4. Too expensive   (   )
    5. These schemes are not for
       people like me   (   )
    6. These schemes are corrupt   (   )
    0. Other (specify) ....

Ask only if married, if not→ Q 419

416. Would you go abroad with your spouse, or would s/he stay here?
    1. Spouse would stay here   (   )
    2. Go with spouse → **Q418**   (   )
    3. Spouse already abroad → **Q419** (   )
    8. Don't know → **Q419**   (   )

417. Why would your spouse stay here?
    1. Better financially   (   )
    2. Family farm/business would
       need to be maintained   (   )
    3. Better for children/family at home (   )
    4. Spouse not permitted to go   (   )
    5. Would want to find out how things
       would work first   (   )
    0. Other (specify) .... **Now → Q419**

(continued)

418. Why would your spouse go with you?
    1. Better financially   (   )
    2. Would need help abroad   (   )
    3. Better for family/children
       to be together   (   )
    0. Other (specify) .... (   )

419. What job would you expect to do there if you go?
    [Ask about WORKPLACE TYPE, WORK TYPE and work level]
    [Insert three lists from explanatory notes if this will help interviewer]

    ....

    ....

    ....

    ....

    ....

    ....

420. Do you speak (name official language of MLD)?
    1. Fluent   (   )
    2. Fairly well   (   )
    3. Neither well nor badly   (   )
    3. Fairly badly   (   )
    4. Not at all   (   )

421. Do you feel you have sufficient information about (name MLD)?
    1. Yes   (   )
    2. No → **Q424**   (   )

422. What were your sources of information?
    [Select up to **three** sources **in the order they are mentioned**]
    1. I have been there   (   )
    2. Family/friends in (name MLD)   (   )
    3. Family/friends in
       (name survey country)   (   )
    4. TV/radio   (   )
    5. Internet   (   )
    6. Newspapers/books/magazines (   )
    7. School/university   (   )
    8. Agencies/institutions/organizations
       in (name MLD)   (   )
    9. Agencies/institutions/organizations
       in (name survey country)   (   )
    0. Other (specify) .... (   )

423. What was the most useful source of information?

    ....

424. Do you plan to get more information about (name MLD) before you go?
 1. Yes   (   )
 2. No → **Q426**   (   )

425. What sources of information do you have access to?
 1. I have been there   (   )
 2. Family/friends in (name MLD)   (   )
 3. Family/friends in
    (name survey country)   (   )
 4. TV/radio   (   )
 5. Internet   (   )
 6. Newspapers/books/magazines   (   )
 7. School/university   (   )
 8. Agencies/institutions/organizations
    in (name MLD)   (   )
 9. Agencies/institutions/organizations i
    n (name survey country)   (   )
 0. Other (specify)   (   )

426. Would you attend any training here in (name survey country) specifically to prepare for living
 or working abroad?
 1. Yes   (   )
 2. No → **Q428**   (   )
 8. Don't know → **Q428**   (   )

427. What kind of training would you do?
 1. Language training   (   )
 2. Cultural orientation   (   )
 3. Vocational training (specify)   (   ) ....
 4. University studies   (   )
 0. Other (specify) ....
 8. Don't know   (   )

428. What kind of official documents do you need to go to (name MLD)?

	MENTIONED	NOT MENTIONED	DO YOU HAVE ALREADY?		HAVE ALREADY	NOT MENTIONED
			YES	NO		
1. Passport	1	2	1	2	....	....
2. Visa for entering (name MLD)	1	2	1	2	....	....
3. Immunization / health certificate	1	2	1	2	....	....
4. Work Contract	1	2	1	2	....	....
5. Approval certificate for study or training from concerned Organization	1	2	1	2	....	....
0. Other (specify)	1	2	1	2	....	....
8. Don't know → **Q 430**	1	2	1	2	....	....

(continued)

429. Do you think you will have difficulty in getting the rest?
    1. Yes   (   )
    2. No   (   )
    8. Don't know   (   )

430. How long do you think you are likely to stay in (name MLD)?
    1. Less than 1 year   (   )
    2. 1-2 years   (   )
    3. 3-5 years   (   )
    4. 5-10 years   (   )
    5. >10 years but not forever (   )
    6. Forever → **Q433**   (   )

431. After that time, do you think you will come home or go to another country?
    1. Return home → **Q433**   (   )
    2. Move to another country   (   )
    8. Don't know   (   )

432. Do you ever expect to return home?
    1. Yes   (   )
    2. Maybe   (   )
    3. No   (   )
    8. Don't know   (   )

433. If you go abroad, would you expect to send money home?
    1. Yes   (   )
    2. No → **Q435**   (   )
    8. Don't know → **Q435**   (   )

434. What would the money be for?
    1. Living expenses   (   )
    2. To buy property   (   )
    3. To rent property   (   )
    4. To buy furniture/household goods (   )
    5. For a business activity   (   )
    6. Savings   (   )
    7. Education   (   )
    0. Other (specify) ....
    8. Don't know   (   )

435. Do you think that your experiences abroad will help you find better work opportunities when you return?
    1. Yes   (   )
    2. No   (   )
    8. Don't know   (   )

436. Do you think that you will be better or worse off when you return than now?
    1. Much better off   (   )
    2. Better off   (   )
    3. About the same   (   )

4. Worse off   (   )
5. Much worse off   (   )

Section E. Economic and living conditions of household

501. How many people are living in this household? ....persons
      (note: include those who are temporarily absent)

502. Are all of these people currently living in [name survey country], or are any of them
      currently living outside [name survey country]?
      1. All in [name survey country]   (   ) → **Q504**
      2. Some outside   (   )

503. How many are living in:
      1. EU countries _____
      2. Other European countries (incl. Ukraine, Russia, Turkey) _____
      3. Middle East (includes all Arab countries, plus Israel) _____
      4. USA and Canada _____
      0. Other (specify) .... _____

504. Type of housing [Prompt: write in, don't ask]
      1. House   (   )
      2. Apartment   (   )
      0. Other (specify) ....

505. Do you own or rent your house or apartment?
      1. Own   (   )
      2. Rent   (   )
      3. Live in free of charge   (   )

506. How many rooms do you have? _____ rooms (exclude kitchen and bathrooms)

507. Do you have access to any of the following (read each – code yes/no):
      Yes No
      1. Hot water 1 2
      2. Radio 1 2
      3. TV 1 2
      4. Automatic washing machine 1 2
      5. Motorcycle 1 2
      6. Car 1 2
      7. Refrigerator 1 2
      8. Butagaz Oven 1 2
      9. Toilet inside the home 1 2
      10. Piped drinking water inside the house 1 2

508. Do you have any income or benefit from any of the following (read each, code yes/no):
      Yes No
      1. Rental on property 1 2
      2. Agriculture 1 2

(continued)

3. Interest on savings 1 2
4. Social assistance/pension 1 2
5. Work of other family members in [name survey country] 1 2
6. Remittances from somebody living and working abroad 1 2
0. Other (specify) 1 2

509. Do you own agricultural land? *[ask all respondents]*
    1. Yes   (   )
    2. No   (   ) → **Q511**

510. How much agricultural land does this household own?
    .... Karate .... Feddan [service providers to include appropriate units]

511. In the last 12 months, how often did you receive money from someone abroad? *[ask all]*
    1. Once a month or more   (   )
    2. Less than once a month, but more
       than once over the whole year   (   )
    3. Only once   (   )
    4. Not at all in the last
       12 months → **Q513**   (   )

512. About how much money did you receive in the last 12 months?
    .... Pounds/Dinars/Lek/Lei
    .... Euros

513. Overall, is the financial situation of the household sufficient to cover all your basic needs?
    1. More than sufficient   (   )
    2. Sufficient   (   )
    3. Sometimes sufficient,
       sometimes not   (   )
    4. Insufficient   (   )
    5. Not at all sufficient   (   )   See explanatory notes

514. How would you rate this household economically compared to other households in this neighbourhood?
    1. Much better off   (   )
    2. Better off   (   )
    3. The same   (   )
    4. Worse off   (   )
    5. Much worse off   (   )   See explanatory notes

Thank respondent and end interview

Return Migration Survey

Serial No. ....

Interviewee Name: ....

Gender: 1. Male   (   )   2. Female (   )

Governorate / District: .... City / Village: ....

Relationship to Head of Household

        1. Head of household   (   )   2. Spouse of HHH   (   )

        3. Son/Daughter of HHH (   )   4. Grandson/daughter of HHH (   )

        0. Other   (   )

Interview Date: /   / 2006

Researcher Name: ....

Field Supervisor Name: ....

**All information provided is confidential and will
be used only for research purposes**

Introduction

This research is being conducted by ETF, an agency of the European Union. The purpose is to understand the link between migration and the labour market education and training. The results will be used for information for the development of migration and education policies. We would like to talk to you to find out your experience and opinions related to travelling abroad for work. Whatever we hear from you will only be used for the purposes of this research.

Section A. Social and Demographic Characteristics and Education

108.   How old are you? _____ _____ years

109.   What is your current marital status?
      1. Never married   (   )
      2. Engaged   (   )
      3. Married   (   )
      4. Widowed   (   )
      5. Divorced   (   )

110.   Do you have any children?
      1. Yes
      2. No **→ Q105**

111.   How many? _____ child(ren)

(continued)

112. What is the highest level of education you have completed?
    1. Did not attend school   (   ) → **Q108**
    2. Less than Primary   (   ) → **Q108**
    3. Primary   (   ) → **Q108**
    4. Preparatory/post-primary   (   ) → **Q108**   See explanatory notes
    5. Secondary General   (   )
    6. Secondary Vocational   (   )
    7. Post-secondary   (   )
    8. University   (   )

113. What was your field of study?
    [to be coded according to ISCED fields after completion of interview]
    ....

114. Why did you choose this field of study? [choose one reason only]
    1. Personal interest   (   )
    2. Encouraged by others   (   )
    3. To get a job   (   )
    4. To be able to go abroad   (   )
    5. Because of the grades I obtained   (   )
    0. Other (specify)   (   )

108. Do you think that education helps people to improve their living standards?
    1. Yes   (   )
    2. No   (   )
    8. Don't know   (   )

109. Do you think it is important to invest in education?
    1. Yes   (   )
    2. No   (   )
    8. Don't know   (   )

110. What language did you speak at home as a child?
    ....

112. Besides this language, which other languages do you speak?
    1. None
    2. English
    3. French
    4. Russian
    5. Italian
    6. Greek
    7. Arabic
    8. Romanian
    0. Other (specify) ....

Section B. Migration History

I would now like to ask you some questions about your time abroad.

201. How long did you live abroad? .... month .... year
(Note: record years, then months. **If <6 months, end interview)**

202. When did you return? .... month .... year
(Note: record date. If <3 months or>10 years ago, end interview)

203. Please give me your reasons for leaving (name survey country)
[List up to **three** reasons **in the order they are mentioned**]
[if left more than once, answer about the **last** time you went abroad
for more than six months]
[insert list from explanatory notes if this will help interviewer]
....
....

204. What was your most important reason?
....
....

205. Would you say the decision to move abroad was made by you or by others?
1. Entirely yours   (   ) →**Q207**
2. Made entirely by others   (   )
3. Both   (   )
8. Do not know   (   ) →**Q207**

206. Who were involved in influencing your decision?
1. Parents   (   )
2. Spouse   (   )
3. Brothers/sisters   (   )
4. In-laws   (   )
5. Employer   (   )
6. Friend   (   )
0. Other (specify) ....

207. Did you attend any training before you went abroad specifically to prepare you
for living or working abroad?
1. Language training   (   )
2. Cultural orientation   (   )
3. Vocational training   (   )
4. University studies   (   )
5. Did not attend training   (   ) → **Q211**
0. Other (specify) ....

208. Did you receive a diploma or certificate from this training?
1. Yes   (   )
2. No   (   )

(continued)

209. Was this training useful in order to get a job abroad?
    1. Yes it was useful   (   )
    2. It was not useful   (   )

210. Was this training _necessary_ in order to get a job abroad
    1. Yes it was necessary   (   )
    2. No, it was not necessary   (   )

211. Did you live abroad in one country, or more than one country?
    1. One country   (   )
    2. More than one country   (   )

212. Which country did you   (first) move to when you went abroad?
    .... [=FDC]   (do not include countries in which you spent
                                              <6 months)

213. How long did you spend there? .... month .... year

214. Why did you move to (name FDC) in particular?
    [List up to **three** reasons **in the order they are mentioned**]
    [insert list from explanatory notes if this will help interviewer]
    ....
    ....

215. What was the most important reason?
    ....
    ....

216. At the time you left, were you aware of any government programmes or companies
    that helped people to work abroad?
    1. Government programmes   (   )
    2. Private recruitment companies   (   )
    3. Both of the above   (   )
    4. No ➔ **Q218**   (   )

217. Did you participate in any of these programmes or use these companies?
    1. Yes, only government scheme   (   ) ➔ **Q219**
    2. Yes, only private company   (   ) ➔ **Q219**
    3. Yes, both   (   ) ➔ **Q219**
    4. No   (   )

218. Why did you not benefit from a programme or use a company?
    1. Not for the right kind of work   (   )
    2. I did not have the required
        qualifications   (   )
    3. No schemes for the country I went to (   )
    4. Too expensive   (   )
    5. These schemes are not for people
        like me   (   )
    6. These schemes are corrupt   (   )
    0. Other (specify) ....

219. **[Ask only if married]** Did you go to FDC with your spouse, or did s/he stay here?
    1. Spouse stayed here   (   )
    2. Went with spouse   (   ) → **Q221**

220. Why did your spouse stay here?
    1. Better financially   (   )
    2. Family farm/business needed
       to be maintained   (   )
    3. Better for children/family at home   (   )
    4. Spouse not permitted to go   (   )
    5. Wanted to find out how things
       would work first   (   )
    6. They were not married at the time   (   )
    0. Other (specify) .... → **Q 222**

221. Why did you bring your spouse with you?
    1. Better financially   (   )
    2. Needed help abroad   (   )
    3. Better for family/children to be
       together   (   )
    0. Other (specify) ....

222. What is the country you have spent most time in abroad?
    .... [=MDC]

223. How long did you spend there? .... month .... year

224. When you lived in (name MDC), did you live in an area where a lot of migrants live?
    1. Almost all migrants   (   )
    2. Mostly migrants   (   )
    3. Equal numbers of migrants
       and locals   (   )
    4. Mostly locals   (   )
    5. Hardly any migrants at all   (   )   See explanatory notes

225. Did you have much contact with local people?
    1. Very frequent contact   (   )
    2. Frequent   (   )
    3. Neither frequent nor infrequent   (   )
    4. Not much/barely   (   )
    5. None at all   (   )   See explanatory notes

226. Did you study or attend training abroad?
    1. Yes   (   )
    2. No   (   ) → **Q228**

227. What kind of study or training did you complete abroad?
    1. University   (   )
    2. Orientation training   (   )
    3. Language training   (   )

(continued)

4. Training to bring existing
   qualifications up to local standards   (   )
5. Workplace training   (   )
0. Other (specify) ....

228. What was the _first_ work you did when you were abroad? [i.e. in FDC]
     [Ask about work place type, work type and work level)
     [Insert three lists from explanatory notes if this will help interviewer]
     ....
     ....
     ....
     ....
     ....
     ....

229. For how long did you do this work? .... month .... year

230. Did you change and do another job while you were abroad?
     1. Yes   (   )
     2. No   (   ) → **Q232**

231. What work did you do for the _longest time_ abroad? [i.e. in MDC]
     [Ask about work place type, work type and work level)
     [Insert three lists from explanatory notes if this will help interviewer]
     ....
     ....
     ....
     ....
     ....
     ....

232. Was there ever a period when you were abroad when you could not find any work?
     1. Yes   (   )
     2. No   (   ) → **Q234**

233. For how many months, approximately, were you without work? .... months

234. On average, about how many hours did you normally work per week when you were abroad?
     [answer in relation to _longest period_ of work, even if part-time] .... hours

235. Did you keep contact with (name survey country) whilst you were abroad?
     1. Yes   (   )
     2. No   (   )

236. How frequently did you visit (name survey country) whilst you were in (name MDC)?
     1. Never   (   )
     2. Once only   (   )
     3. From time to time   (   )
     4. At least once a year   (   )
     5. More than once a year   (   )

237. Did you send money home whilst you were abroad?
   1. Yes   (   )
   2. No   (   ) → **Q301**

238. How often did you send money?
   1. Less than once a year   (   )
   2. At least once a year   (   )
   3. At least once a month   (   )

239. Who did you send the money to?
   1. Parent(s)   (   )
   2. Spouse   (   )
   3. Children   (   )
   4. Siblings   (   )
   0. Other (specify) ....

240. What was the money used for?
   1. Living expenses   (   )
   2. To buy property   (   )
   3. To rent property   (   )
   4. To buy furniture/household goods (   )
   5. For a business activity   (   )
   6. Savings   (   )
   7. Education   (   )
   0. Other (specify) ....

Section C. Return experiences

I'd now like to ask you some questions about the period since you last returned to (name survey country)

301. Talking about your return to (name survey country), please give me the reasons for your return:
   [insert list from explanatory notes if this will help interviewer]
   [List up to **three** reasons **in the order they are mentioned**
   ....
   ....

302. What was the most important reason?
   ....
   ....

303. At the time you returned, were you aware of any official programmes or schemes to assist people to return?
   1. Yes   (   )
   2. No   (   ) → **Q306**

304. Did you benefit from such a scheme?
   1. Yes (specify)   (   ) .... →**Q306**
   2. No   (   )

(continued)

305. Why not?
     1. Not for the right kind of work   (   )
     2. I did not have the required
        qualifications   (   )
     3. No schemes for the country I went to   (   )
     5. Too expensive   (   )
     6. These schemes are not for
        people like me   (   )
     7. These schemes are corrupt   (   )
     0. Other (specify) ....

306. When you came back, did you bring money/savings with you?
     1. Yes   (   )
     2. No   (   ) → **Q308**

307. What did you use these savings for?
     1. Living expenses   (   )
     2. To buy property   (   )
     3. To rent property   (   )
     4. To buy furniture/household goods   (   )
     5. For a business activity   (   )
     6. Savings   (   )
     7. Education   (   )
     0. Other (specify) ....

308. Have you worked since you came back to (name survey country)?
     1. Yes   (   )
     2. No   (   ) → **Q316**

309. What work have you done since you returned?
     [Prompt if more than one job/activity to describe main job/activity only here – i.e. job
     done for the longest time]
     [Insert three lists from explanatory notes if this will help interviewer]
     ....
     ....
     ....
     ....
     ....
     ....

310. On average, how many hours do you normally work each week since you returned?
     .... hours

311. How did you find work?
     1. Advertisement   (   )
     2. Offered a job by a friend or relative   (   )
     3. Asked/sent CV to a number
        of employers   (   )
     4. Set up own business   (   )
     5. Returned to their original job   (   )
     0. Other (specify) ....

312. How quickly did you start work after arrival   (excluding any periods you chose to take
     time off)?

     0. On arrival
     .... months

313. Have your experiences abroad helped you find better work opportunities since
     your return?
     1. Yes   (   )
     2. No   (   ) → **Q315**

314. Of all your experiences abroad, which have helped you most?
     1. Experiences in general   (   )
     2. Formal education/training   (   )
     3. Skills learned at work   (   )
     0. Other (specify) ....
     → **Q316**

315. Why have your experiences abroad not helped you?
     ....
     ....

316. Do you have a pension or other social benefits from your time abroad?
     1. Yes   (   ) → **Q318**
     2. No   (   )

317. Why not?
     1. Did not contribute to
        pension scheme   (   )
     2. Contributed, but not for a long
        enough period   (   )
     3. Pension scheme could not
        be transferred   (   )
     4. There were no such
        benefits/schemes   (   )
     0. Other (specify) ....

318. When compared to the time before you left, do you consider yourself better or worse
     off since your return?
     1. Much better off than before you left   (   )
     2. Better off than before you left   (   )
     3. About the same as before you left   (   )
     4. Worse off than before you left   (   )
     5. Much worse off than before you left   (   )   See explanatory notes

319. In what way do you feel better/worse off?
     ....
     ....

(continued)

....

Section D. Intentions

401. Are you currently considering moving abroad to live and work again?
    1. Yes   (   ) → **Q404**
    2. No   (   )

402. Why are you not looking to move abroad?
    [Select up to **three** reasons **in the order they are mentioned**]
    1. This is my country/I belong here   (   )
    2. My family/relatives are here   (   )
    3. People are not friendly abroad   (   )
    4. Discrimination in other countries   (   )
    5. I would feel lonely abroad   (   )
    6. Homesickness   (   )
    7. Low incomes abroad   (   )
    8. Poor work conditions abroad   (   )
    9. Impossible or very difficult to
       find work abroad   (   )
    0. Other (specify) ....

403. What is the most important reason?
    ....
    ....

    → **Q501**

404. How likely or unlikely is it that you would leave (name survey country) within the next
    <u>6 months</u>?
    1. Very unlikely   (   ) See explanatory notes
    2. Quite unlikely   (   )
    3. Neither likely nor unlikely   (   )
    4. Quite likely   (   )
    5. Very likely   (   ) → **also tick 'very likely' to Q405**

405. How likely or unlikely is it that you would leave (name survey country) within the next
    <u>2 years</u>?
    1. Very unlikely   (   ) See explanatory notes
    2. Quite unlikely   (   )
    3. Neither likely nor unlikely   (   )
    4. Quite likely   (   )
    5. Very likely   (   )

406. If you were to leave (name survey country), please give me the reasons you would
    have for leaving?
    [insert list from explanatory notes if this will help interviewer]
    [List up to **three** reasons **in the order they are mentioned**]
    ....
    ....

407. What is your most important reason?

....

....

408. If you were to move abroad, which country would you be most likely to go to?
.... [=MLD]

409. How likely or unlikely is it that you would move to (name MLD) to live and work?
1. Very unlikely   (   )
2. Quite unlikely   (   )
3. Neither likely nor unlikely   (   )
4. Quite likely   (   )
4. Very likely   (   )   See explanatory notes

410. Why would you move to (name MLD)?
[insert list from explanatory notes if this will help interviewer]
[List up to **three** reasons **in the order they are mentioned**]

....

....

411. What is the most important reason?

....

....

412. Are you able to finance your move abroad?
1. Yes   (   )
2. No   (   )
8. Don't know   (   )

413. What job would you expect to do there if you go?
[Ask about work place type, work type and work level)
[Insert three lists from explanatory notes if this will help interviewer]

....

....

....

....

....

....

Section E. Economic and living conditions of household

501. How many people are living in this household? .... persons
(note: include those who are temporarily absent)

502. Are all of these people currently living in [name survey country], or are any of them currently living outside
[name survey country?]
1. All in [name survey country]   (   ) → **Q504**
2. Some outside   (   )

503. How many are living in:
1. EU countries ....

(continued)

2. Other European countries (includes Ukraine, Russia, Turkey)   ....
3. Middle East (includes all Arab countries and Israel)   ....
4. USA and Canada   ....
5. Other (specify) ....

504. Type of housing [Prompt: write in, don't ask]
      1. House   (   )
      2. Apartment   (   )
      0. Other (specify) ....

505. Do you own or rent your house or apartment?
      1. Own   (   )
      2. Rent   (   )
      3. Live in free of charge   (   )

506. How many rooms do you have? .... rooms   (exclude entrance hall, kitchen
                                                                 and
                                                                 bathrooms)

507. Do you have access to any of the following (read each – code yes/no):
      Yes No
      1. Hot water 1 2
      2. Radio 1 2
      3. TV 1 2
      4. Automatic washing machine 1 2
      5. Motorcycle 1 2
      6. Car 1 2
      7. Refrigerator 1 2
      8. Botagaz oven 1 2
      9. Toilet inside the home 1 2
      10. Piped drinking water inside the house 1 2

508. Do you have any income or benefit from any of the following (read each, code yes/no):
      Yes No
      1. Rental on property 1 2
      2. Agriculture 1 2
      3. Interest on savings 1 2
      4. Social assistance/pension 1 2
      5. Work of other family members in [name survey country] 1 2
      6. Remittances from somebody living and working abroad **1 2**
      0. Other (specify) 1 2

509. Do you own agricultural land? *[ask all respondents]*
      1. Yes   (   )
      2. No   (   ) **→ Q511**

510. How much agricultural land does this household own?

      .... Karate .... Feddan [service providers to include
      appropriate units]

511. In the last 12 months, how often did you receive money from someone abroad?

1. Once a month or more   (   )
2. Less than once a month, but more
   than once over the whole year   (   )
3. Only once   (   )
4. Not at all in the last 12 months
   → **Q513**   (   )

512. About how much money did you receive in the last 12 months?
     .... Pounds/Dinars/Lek/Lei
     .... Euros

513. Overall, is the financial situation of the household sufficient to cover all your basic needs?
     1. More than sufficient   (   )
     2. Sufficient   (   )
     3. Sometimes sufficient, sometimes not   (   )
     4. Insufficient   (   )
     5. Not at all sufficient   (   )   See explanatory notes

514. How would you rate this household economically compared to other households in this neighbourhood?
     1. Much better off   (   )
     2. Better off   (   )
     3. The same   (   )
     4. Worse off   (   )
     5. Much worse off   (   )   See explanatory notes

Thank respondent and end interview

References

Acosta, P. 1987. "Self-Selection and the Earnings of Immigrants." *American Economic Review* 77 (531–553).

———. 2005. "The German 'green card'." *Focus Migration* Policy Brief (November). http://www.focus-migration.de/uploads/tx_wilpubdb/PB03_-_Green_Card.pdf

———. 2006a. "Labour Supply, School Attendance, and Remittances from International Immigration: The Case of El Salvador." Policy Research Working Paper 3903, World Bank, Washington, DC.

———. 2006b. "Remittances, Poverty, and Investment in Guatemala." In *International Migration, Remittances, and the Brain Drain*, ed. Ç. Özden and M. Schiff. Washington, DC: World Bank and Palgrave Macmillan.

———. 2006c. "Migration Management Between Europe, the Middle East, and North Africa: Demographic trends, labour force projections, and the consequences for policies of immigration, social protection, and labour market institutions." MENA report, World Bank, Washington DC.

———. 2007. "Brain circulation and knowledge society in the Mediterranean Region." In *Mediterranean Yearbook 2007*, IEMed and Fundaciò CIDOB.

Acosta, P., P. Fajnzylber, and J. H. López. 2007. "The Impact of Remittances on Poverty and Human Resources: Evidence from Latin American Households Survey." In *International Migration, Economic Development and Policy*, ed. Ç. Özden and M. Schiff. Washington, DC: World Bank and Palgrave Macmillan.

Adams, R.H. 2003. "International Migration, Remittances and the Brain Drain: A Study of 24 Labour-Exporting Countries." Policy Research Working Paper 3069, World Bank, Washington, DC.

Alvarez-Plata, P., H. Brücker, and B. Siliverstovs. 2003. *Potential Migration from Central and Eastern Europe into the EU-15—An Update.* European Commission, DG Employment and Social Affairs Consultant Report, DIW Berlin.

Aminuzamman, S.M. 2007. *Migration of Skilled Nurses from Bangladesh,* DRC Research Report, Development Research Centre on Migration, Globalisation and Poverty, University of Sussex, Brighton.

Arab League. 2004. *Arab Migration in a Globalised World.* Publication of the proceedings of a regional conference organized by League of Arab States and International Organization for Migration, Cairo, Egypt, September 2–4, 2003.

Avato, J. 2009. "Migration Pressures and Immigration Policies: New Evidence on the Selection of Migrants." Social Protection Discussion Paper. World Bank, Washington, DC.

Baldwin-Edwards, M. 2005. *Migration in the Middle East and Mediterranean.* Global Commission on International Migration, Geneva.

Bardak, U. 2006. "Understanding the dynamics between migration, skills and poverty reduction in the Mediterranean Region." In *ETF Yearbook 2006–Skills Development for Poverty Reduction.* ETF, Turin.

Black, R. and E. Markova. 2007. *East European Immigration and Community Cohesion.* London: Joseph Rowntree Foundation.

Black, R., R. King, and R. Tiemoko. 2003. "Migration, return and small enterprise development in Ghana: a route out of poverty?" Migration Working Paper 9. University of Sussex, Brighton.

Borjas, G. 1991. "Immigration and Self-Selection." In *Immigration, Trade and the Labor Market,* ed. J. Abowd and R. Freeman. Chicago: Chicago University Press: Chicago.

Boubakri, H. 2004. *Transit migration between Tunisia, Libya and Sub-Saharan Africa: study based on greater Tunis.* Council of Europe, Strasbourg.

Brozozowsky, J. 2008. "Brain Drain or Brain Gain? The New Economics of Brain Drain Reconsidered." Social Science Research Network. http://ssrn.com/abstract =1288043

Cassarino, J-.P. 2006. "The EU return policy: premises and implications." MIREM Return Migration in Maghreb Project, MIREM/ EUI Working Paper. European University Institute, Florence.

Castles, S., and R. Delgado Wise. 2008. *Migration and Development: Perspectives from the South.* International Organization for Migration, Geneva.

CBS-AXA. 2005. *Migration and Remittances in Moldova.* Report prepared for the International Organization for Migration mission in Moldova, European Commission Food Security Programme Office in Moldova, and International Monetary Fund Office in Moldova.

CEDEFOP (European Centre for the Development of Vocational Training). 2008. *Future Skill Needs in Europe. Medium-Term Forecast. Synthesis Report.* Luxembourg: Office for Official Publications of the European Communities.

Chiquiar, D., and G.H. Hanson. 2005. "International Migration, Self-Selection, and the Distribution of Wages: Evidence from Mexico and the United States." Journal of Political Economy 113 (2).

Chiswick, B. 1978. "The Effect of Americanization on the Earnings of Foreign-Born Men." *Journal of Political Economy* 86 (5): 897–921.

———. 2000. "Are immigrants favourably selected? An economic analysis." IZA DP 131. Bonn.

Collyer, M. 2004. "The Development Impact Of Temporary International Labour Migration Schemes: Contrasting Examples Of Morocco And Egypt." Working Paper WPT6, Development Research Centre on Migration, Globalisation and Poverty. University of Sussex, Brighton.

Constant, A., and D. Massey. 2003. "Self-Selection, Earnings, And Out-Migration: A Longitudinal Study Of Immigrants To Germany." *Journal of Population Economics* 16 (4): 631–653.

Craciun, C. 2006. *Migration and remittances in the Republic of Moldova: empirical evidence at a micro-level.* Kiev: National University Kyiv-Mohyla Academy.

De Rosa, D., and C. Uregian. 2008. "Moldova: Building the Microeconomic Foundations for Private Sector Competitiveness." Technical Note, ECSPF, World Bank.

de Zwager, N., Gedeshi, E. Germenji, and C. Nikas. 2005. *Competing for remittances.* International Organization for Migration and Albanian Government, Tirana.

Docquier, F., and A. Marfouk. 2006. "International Migration by Educational Attainment." In *International Migration, Remittances and the Brain Drain,* ed. Ç. Özden and M. Schiff. Washington, DC: World Bank and Palgrave Macmillan.

ETF (European Training Foundation). 2007a. "The Contribution Of Human Resources Development To Migration Policy In Albania." http://www.etf.europa.eu

———. 2007b. "The Contribution Of Human Resources Development To Migration Policy In Egypt." http://www.etf.europa.eu

———. 2007c. "The Contribution Of Human Resources Development To Migration Policy In Moldova." http://www.etf.europa.eu

————. 2008. "The Contribution Of Human Resources Development To Migration Policy In Ukraine." http://www.etf.europa.eu

————. 2009a. "Black Sea Labour Market Reviews—Moldova Country Report." Eskola, E. 2007. "Investing In A Brighter Future Abroad? The Need To Create A Domestic Alternative In Moldova. An Integrated Economic Analysis Approach." SIDA, Chisinau.

————. 2009b. "Black Sea Labour Market Reviews—Ukraine Country Report." http://www.etf.europa.eu

Fargues, P. 2005. *Mediterranean Migration–2005 Report*. EUI-RSCAS, CARIM Consortium, Florence.

Fassmann, H., and C. Hintermann. 1997. *Migrationspotential Ostmitteleuropa: Struktur und Motivation potentieller Migranten aus Polen, der Slowakei, Tschechien und Ungarn*, ISR-Forschungsberichte 15. Vienna, Austria: Verlag der Osterreichischen Akademie der Wissenschaften.

Government of Albania. 2004. *National Strategy on Migration*. Albanian Government and International Organization for Migration, Tirana.

Gubert, F., and C. Nordman. 2008. "Who Benefits Most From Migration? An Empirical Analysis Using Data On Return Migrants In The Maghreb." MIREM-AR 2008/3 Analytical Report. Joint-funded project by EU, EIU, and World Bank.

Hagen-Zanker, J., and M. Siegel. 2007. "The Determinants Of Remittances: A Comparison Between Albania And Moldova." Maastricht Graduate School of Governance Working Paper. http://www.governance.unimaas.nl/home/staff/research_fellows/jessica_hagen_zanker/Hagenzanker_Siegel_2007_short.pdf

Holzmann, R., and R. Münz. 2004. *Challenges and Opportunities of International Migration for the EU, Its Member States, Neighboring Countries and Regions: A Policy Note*. Stockholm: Institute for Future Studies.

Ivlevs, A. 2008. "Are Ethnic Minorities More Likely To Emigrate? Evidence from Latvia." Research Paper 2008/11, University of Nottingham. http://www.gep.org.uk/shared/shared_levpublications/Research_Papers/2008/2008_11.pdf

King, R., M. Dalipaj, and N. Mai. 2007. "Gendering Migration And Remittances: Evidence From Northern Albania." *Population, Place and Space* 12 (6): 409–434.

Koettl, J. 2005. *What Types of Migrants Will Europe Need and What Will the Mediterranean Be Able to Offer? Education and Age Structure of the Population and Labour Force Around the Mediterranean Basin Until 2050*. World Bank, Washington DC.

Kule, D., A. Mançellari, H. Papapanagos, S. Qirici, and P. Sanfey. 2000. *The causes and consequences of Albanian emigration during transition: evidence from micro data*. European Bank for Reconstruction and Development, London.

Lianos, T.P., and J. Cavoundis. 2004. "Immigrant remittances, stability of employment and relative deprivation." Paper presented at the New

Perspectives on Albanian Migration and Development, Korçë, Albania, September 16–17.

Mansoor, A., and B. Quillin. 2007. *Migration and Remittances: Eastern Europe and the Former Soviet Union.* World Bank, Washington, DC.

Martin, P.L., and J.E. Taylor. 1996. "The anatomy of a migration hump." In *Development Strategy, Employment and Migration: Insights from Models,* ed. J.E. Taylor. OECD Development Centre, Paris.

McCormick, B., and J. Wahba. 2003. "Return international migration and geographical inequality: The case of Egypt." *Journal of African Economies* 12 (4): 500–532.

Mesnard, A. 2004. "Temporary migration and capital market imperfections." Oxford Economic Papers 56.

Ministero del Interno. 2007. *Primo rapporto sugli immigrati in Italia.* Rome.

Mora, J., and J. E. Taylor. 2005. "Determinants of Migration, Destination, and Sector Choice: Disentangling Individual, Household, and Community Effects." In *International Migration, Remittances, and the Brain Drain,* ed. Ç. Özden and M. Schiff. Washington DC: World Bank and Palgrave Macmillan.

Munteanu, A. 2001. "Moldova without Moldovans: labour emigration—a loss or a gain?" *South-East Europe Review* 4: 19–24.

Namsuk, K. 2007. "The Impact of Remittances on Labour Supply: The Case of Jamaica." World Bank Policy Research Working Paper 4120.

OECD. 2004a. *Migration for employment. bilateral agreements at a crossroads.* OECD, Paris.

———. 2004b. *Trends in international migration.* OECD, Paris.

———. 2007. *Policy coherence for development: migration and developing countries.* OECD, Paris.

Palloni, A., D.S. Massey, M. Ceballos, K. Espinosa, and M. Spittel. 2001. "Social Capital and International Migration: A Test Using Information on Family Networks." *American Journal of Sociology* 106 (5): 1262–1298.

Pantiru, C., R. Black, and R. Sabates-Wheeler. 2007. "Migration and poverty reduction in Moldova." Working Paper WPC10, Development Research Centre on Migration, Globalisation and Poverty, University of Sussex, Brighton.

Rangelova, R., and K. Vladimirova. 2004. "Migration from Central and Eastern Europe: the case of Bulgaria." *South East Europe Review* 3: 7–30. http://www.ceeol.com/aspx/getdocument.aspx?logid=5&id=6EFAC8FC-DA9B-4569-8B09-FF860A861AFD

Ruiz, N.G. 2008. "Managing migration: lessons from the Philippines." Migration and Development Brief of the World Bank, Migration and Remittances Team.

Rutkowski, J. 2004. "Firms, jobs and employment in Moldova." Policy Research Working Paper 3253, World Bank, Washington, DC.

Saleh, M.A. 2006. "Migration Statistics Situation in Egypt." Paper presented at Joint UNECE/Eurostat Work Session on Migration Statistics, Edinburgh, November 20–22.

———. 2006. "Migration statistics situation in Egypt." Paper presented at the Joint UNECE/Eurostat Work Session on Migration Statistics, Edinburgh, November 20–22. http://www.unece.org/stats/documents/ece/ces/ge.10/2006/wp.28.e.ppt

Schumpeter, J.A. 1975. *Capitalism, Socialism and Democracy.* New York: Harper. Original published 1942.

Skeldon, R. 1997. *Migration and Development: A Global Perspective.* Essex, United Kingdom: Longman.

Stark, O. 2004. "Rethinking the brain drain." *World Development* 32 (1): 15–22.

Stark, O., and J.E. Taylor. 1991. "Migration Incentives, Migration Types: The Role of Relative Deprivation." *The Economic Journal* 101: 1163–1178.

Te Velde, D.W. 2005. "Globalisation and education: what do the trade, investment and migration literatures tell us?" ODI Working Paper, London.

Tunisian Ministry of Higher Education. 2005. *Indicateurs de l'enseignement supérieur.* http://www.universites.tn/francais/indicateurs/ind_fr_mai_2005.pdf

UNDP. 2006. *World Development Indicators 2006.* UNDP, Washington, DC.

Wallace, C. 1999. *Migration potential in Central and Eastern Europe.* International Organization for Migration, Technical Cooperation Centre for Europe and Central Asia, Geneva.

World Bank. 2008. *Migration and Remittances Factbook 2008.* World Bank, Washington, DC.

Zaiceva, A. 2006. "Reconciling the estimates of potential migration into the enlarged European Union." IZA Discussion Paper 2519.

Index

www.ingramcontent.com/pod-product-compliance
Lightning Source LLC
Chambersburg PA
CBHW070926270326
41927CB00011B/2735